LIFE
WITHOUT
LIMITS

INSPIRATION FOR A *RIDICULOUSLY* GOOD LIFE

LIFE
WITHOUT
LIMITS

Bonus:
Personal
Action
Plan

NICK VUJICIC

WATERBROOK
PRESS

Life Without Limits
Published by WaterBrook Press
12265 Oracle Boulevard, Suite 200
Colorado Springs, Colorado 80921

ISBN 978-0-307-58974-3

Originally published in hardcover in slightly different form in the United States by Doubleday Religion, an imprint of the Crown Publishing Group, a division of Random House, Inc., New York, in 2010.

Published in the United States by WaterBrook Multnomah, an imprint of the Crown Publishing Group, a division of Random House Inc., New York.

WaterBrook and its deer colophon are registered trademarks of Random House Inc.

Library of Congress Cataloging-in-Publication Data (hardcover edition)
Vujicic, Nick.
   Life without limits : inspiration for a ridiculously good life / Nick Vujicic. — 1st ed.
     p. cm.
   (alk. paper)
   1. Christian life. 2. Happiness—Religious aspects—Christianity. 3. Vujicic, Nick.
   I. Title.
   BV4501.3.V85 2010
   248.8'6—dc22

                                                   2010020409

Printed in the United States of America
2014

20 19 18 17 16

Special Sales
Most WaterBrook Multnomah books are available at special quantity discounts when purchased in bulk by corporations, organizations, and special-interest groups. Custom imprinting or excerpting can also be done to fit special needs. For information, please e-mail SpecialMarkets@WaterBrookMultnomah.com or call 1-800-603-7051.

Contents

GOD: The Father, Son, and Holy Spirit.
I'd also like to dedicate this book to the Toth family in San Diego, California, as I will never forget the cornerstone of faith Phil placed in my life. His contagious flame for evangelism marked the beginning of mine.

Introduction

My name is Nick Vujicic (pronounced Voy-a-chich). I am twenty-seven years old. I was born without any limbs, but I am not constrained by my circumstances. I travel the world encouraging millions of people to overcome adversity with faith, hope, love, and courage so that they may pursue their dreams. In this book I will share with you my experiences in dealing with adversity and obstacles, some of them unique to me but most universal to us all. My goal is to encourage you to overcome your own challenges and hardships so you can find your *own* purpose and pathway to a ridiculously good life.

Often we feel life is unfair. Hard times and tough circumstances can trigger self-doubt and despair. I understand that well. But the Bible says, "Consider it pure joy, whenever you face trials of any kinds." That is a lesson I struggled many years to learn. I eventually figured it out, and through my experiences I can help you see that most of the hardships we face provide us with opportunities to discover who we are meant to be and what we can share of our gifts to benefit others.

My parents are devout Christians, but after I was born with neither arms nor legs, they wondered what God had in mind in creating me. At first they assumed that there was no hope and no future for someone like me, that I would never live a normal or productive life.

Today, though, my life is beyond anything we could have imagined. Every day I hear from strangers via telephone, e-mail, text, and Twitter. They approach me in airports, hotels, and restaurants and hug me, telling me that I have touched their lives in some way. I am truly blessed. I am *ridiculously* happy.

What my family and I could not foresee was that my disability—my "burden"—could also be a blessing, offering me unique opportunities for reaching out to others, empathizing with them, understanding their pain, and offering them comfort. Yes, I do have distinct challenges, but I also am blessed with a loving family, with a keen enough mind, and with a deep and abiding faith. I'll be candid here and throughout the book in sharing that neither my faith nor my sense of purpose grew strong until I went through some very scary times.

You see, as I entered those difficult adolescent years when we all wonder where we fit in, I despaired over my circumstances, feeling that I never would be "normal." There was no hiding the fact that my body was not like my classmates'. As much as I tried to do ordinary activities like swimming and skateboarding, I would only become more and more aware that there were simply some things I would never be able to do.

It didn't help that a few cruel kids called me a freak and an alien. Of course, I'm all too human and wanted to be like everyone else, but there seemed little chance for that. I wanted to be accepted. I felt I wasn't. I wanted to fit in. It seemed I didn't. And I hit a wall.

My heart ached. I was depressed, overwhelmed with negative thoughts, and didn't see any point in my life. I felt alone even when I was surrounded by family and friends. I worried that I would always be a burden to those I loved.

But I was so, so wrong. What I didn't know back in those dark days could fill a book: the one you're holding, actually. In the pages that follow, I will offer you methods for finding hope even amid arduous trials and heartbreaking tribulations. I'll light the path to the other side of grief where you can emerge stronger, more determined, and empowered to pursue the life you want, and perhaps even to find a life beyond any you could have imagined.

If you have the desire and passion to do something, and it's within God's will, you will achieve it. That's a powerful statement. To be honest, I didn't always believe it myself. If you've seen one of my talks posted on the Internet, the happiness I have that shines through in those videos is the result of the journey I've made. I didn't have everything I needed at first and had to pick up several important attributes along the way. To live without limits, I found I needed:

A powerful sense of purpose

Hope so strong that it cannot be diminished

Faith in God and the infinite possibilities

Love and self-acceptance

Attitude with altitude

A courageous spirit

Willingness to change

A trusting heart

Hunger for opportunities

The ability to assess risks and to laugh at life

A mission to serve others first

Each chapter in this book is devoted to one of those attributes, explained in such a way that I hope you can put them to use in your own journey toward a fulfilling and meaningful life. I'm offering them to you because I share God's love for you. I want you to experience all the joy and fulfillment He intended for you.

If you are one of the many people struggling each day, keep in mind that beyond my own struggles there was a purpose for my life awaiting me. And it has proven to be far, far, *far* beyond anything I ever could have imagined.

You may hit hard times. You may fall down and feel as though you don't have the strength to get back up. I know the feeling, mate. We all do. Life isn't always easy, but when we overcome challenges, we become stronger and more grateful for our opportunities. What really matters are the lives you touch along the way and how you finish your journey.

I love my life just as I love yours. Together, the possibilities for us are just ridiculous. So what do you say? Shall we give it a go, mate?

Life Without Limits

ONE

If You Can't Get a Miracle, Become One

One of my most popular videos on YouTube shows footage of me skateboarding, surfing, playing music, hitting a golf ball, falling down, getting up, speaking to audiences, and best of all, receiving hugs from all sorts of great people.

All in all, those are pretty ordinary activities that just about anybody can do, right? So why do you think that video has been viewed *millions* of times? My theory is that people are drawn to watch it because despite my physical limitations, I'm living as though I have no limits.

People often expect someone with a severe disability to be inactive, maybe even angry and withdrawn. I like to surprise them by showing that I lead a very adventurous and fulfilling existence.

Among the hundreds of comments on that video, here's one typical remark: "Seeing a guy like this being happy makes me wonder why the hell I feel sorry for myself sometimes . . . or feel that I'm not attractive enough, or funny enough, or WHATEVER. How can I even think thoughts like that when this guy is living without limbs and still being HAPPY!?"

I'm often asked that very question: "Nick, how can you be so happy?" You may be dealing with your own challenges, so I'll give you the quick answer up front:

I found happiness when I realized that as imperfect as I may be, I am the perfect Nick Vujicic. I am God's creation, designed according to His plan for me. That's not to say that there isn't room for improvement. I'm always trying to be better so I can better serve Him and the world!

I do believe my life has no limits. I want you to feel the same way about your life, no matter what your challenges may be. As we begin our journey together, please take a moment to think about any limitations you've placed on your life or that you've allowed others to place on it. Now think about what it would be like to be free of those limitations. What would your life be if *anything* were possible?

I'm officially *disabled*, but I'm truly *enabled* because of my lack of limbs. My unique challenges have opened up unique opportunities to reach so many in need. Just imagine what is possible for you!

Too often we tell ourselves we aren't smart enough or attractive enough or talented enough to pursue our dreams. We buy into what others say about us, or we put restrictions on ourselves. What's worse is that when you consider yourself unworthy, you are putting limits on how *God* can work through you!

When you give up on your dreams, you put God in a box. After all, you are His creation. He made you for a purpose. Therefore your life cannot be limited any more than God's love can be contained.

I have a choice. You have a choice. We can choose to dwell on disappointments and shortcomings. We can choose to be bitter, angry, or sad. Or when faced with hard times and hurtful people, we can choose to learn from the experience and move forward, taking responsibility for our own happiness.

As God's child, you are beautiful and precious, worth more than all the diamonds in the world. You and I are perfectly suited to be who we were meant to be! Even still, it should always be our goal to become an even better person and stretch our boundaries by dreaming big. Adjustments are necessary along the way because life isn't always rosy, but it is always worth living. I'm here to tell you that no matter what your circumstances may be, as long as you are breathing, you have a contribution to make.

I can't put a hand on your shoulder to reassure you, but I can speak from the heart. However desperate your life may seem, there is hope. As bad as circumstances appear, there are better days ahead. No matter how dire your circumstances may appear, you can rise above them. To wish for change will change nothing. To make the decision to take action right now will change everything!

All events come together for the good. I'm certain of that because it's been true in my life. What good is a life without limbs? Just by looking at me, people know that I faced and overcame many obstacles and hardships. That makes them willing to listen to me as a source of inspiration. They allow me to share my faith, to tell them they are loved, and to give them hope.

That is my contribution. It's important to recognize your own value. Know that you also have something to contribute. If you feel frustrated right now, that's okay. Your sense of frustration means you want more for your life than you have right now. That's all good. Often it's the challenges in life that show us who we are truly meant to be.

A LIFE OF VALUE

It took me a long time to see the benefits of the circumstances I was born into. My mum was twenty-five years old when she became pregnant with me, her first child. She'd been a midwife and worked as a pediatric nurse in charge in the delivery room where she provided care for hundreds of mothers and their babies. She knew what she had to do while she was pregnant, watching her diet, being cautious about medications, and not consuming alcohol, aspirin, or any other pain-killers. She went to the best doctors and they assured her everything was proceeding smoothly.

Even still, her apprehension persisted. As her due date approached, my mum shared her concerns with my father several times, saying, "I hope that everything's okay with the baby."

When two ultrasounds were performed during her pregnancy, the doctors detected nothing unusual. They told my parents that the baby was a boy but not a word about missing limbs! At my delivery on December 4, 1982, my mother could not see me at first, and the first question she asked the doctor was "Is the baby all right?" There was silence. As the seconds ticked by and they were still not bringing the baby for her to see, she sensed even more that something was wrong. Instead of giving me to my mother to hold, they summoned a pediatrician and moved off to the opposite corner, examining me and conferring with each other. When my mum heard a big healthy baby scream, she was relieved. But my dad, who had noticed I was missing an arm during the delivery, felt queasy and was escorted out of the room.

Shocked at the sight of me, the nurses and doctors quickly wrapped me up.

My mother, who'd participated in hundreds of deliveries as a nurse, wasn't fooled. She read the distress on the faces of her medical team, and she knew something was very wrong.

"What is it? What's wrong with my baby?" she demanded.

Her doctor would not answer at first, but when she insisted on a response, he could offer my mother only a specialized medical term.

"Phocamelia," he said.

Because of her nursing background, my mother recognized the term as the condition babies have when they are born with malformed or missing limbs. She simply couldn't accept that this was true.

In the meantime, my stunned dad was outside, wondering whether he had seen what he thought he saw. When the pediatrician came out to speak to him, he cried out, "My son, he has no arm!"

"Actually," the pediatrician said as sensitively as possible, "your son has neither arms nor legs."

My father went weak with shock and anguish.

He sat stunned, momentarily unable to speak before his protective instincts kicked in. He rushed in to tell my mother before she saw me, but to his dismay he found her lying in bed, crying. The staff had already told her the news. They had offered to bring me to her but she refused to hold me and told them to take me away.

The nurses were crying. The midwife was crying. And of course, I was crying! Finally they put me next to her, still covered, and my mum just couldn't bear what she was seeing: her child without limbs.

"Take him away," she said. "I don't want to touch him or see him."

To this day my father regrets that the medical staff did not give him time to prepare my mother properly. Later, as she slept, he visited me in the nursery. He came back and told Mum, "He looks beautiful." He asked her if she wanted to see me at that point, but she declined, still too shaken. He understood and respected her feelings.

Instead of celebrating my birth, my parents and their whole church mourned. "If God is a God of love," they wondered, "why would He let something like this happen?"

MY MUM'S GRIEF

I was my parents' firstborn child. While this would be a major cause for rejoicing in any family, no one sent flowers to my mum when I was born. This hurt her and only deepened her despair.

Sad and teary-eyed, she asked my dad, "Don't I deserve flowers?"

"I'm sorry," Dad said. "Of course you deserve them." He went to the hospital flower shop and returned shortly to present her with a bouquet.

I was aware of none of this until the age of thirteen or so, when I began to question my parents about my birth and their initial reaction to my lack of limbs. I'd had a bad day at school, and when I told my mum, she cried with me. I told her I was sick of having no arms and legs. She shared my tears and said that she and my dad had come to understand that God had a plan for me and one day He would reveal it. My questions continued over time, sometimes with one parent, sometimes with both. Part of my search for answers was natural curiosity and part of it was in response to the persistent questions I'd been fielding from curious classmates.

At first, I was a little scared of what my parents might tell me, and, since some of this was difficult for them to delve into, I didn't want to put them on the spot. In our initial discussions my mum and dad were very careful and protective in their responses. As I grew older and pushed harder, they offered me deeper insights into their feelings and their fears because they knew I could handle it. Even so, when my mum told me that she didn't want to hold me after I was born, it was hard to take, to say the least. I was insecure enough as it was, but to hear that my own mother could not bear to look at me was . . . well, imagine how you might feel. I was hurt and I felt rejected, but then I thought of all that my parents have done for me since. They'd proven their love many times over. By the time we had these conversations, I was old enough to put myself in her situation. Other than her intuitive feelings, there'd been no warning of this during her pregnancy. She was in shock and frightened. How would I have responded as a parent? I'm not sure I would have handled it as well as they did. I told them that, and over time we went more and more into the details.

I'm glad that we waited until I was secure, knowing deep in my heart of hearts that they loved me. We've continued to share our own feelings and fears, and my parents have helped me understand how their faith enabled them to see that I was destined to serve God's purpose. I was a fiercely determined and mostly upbeat child. My teachers, other parents, and strangers often told my parents that my attitude inspired them. For my part, I came to see that as great as my challenges were, many people had heavier burdens than mine.

Today in my travels around the world, I often see incredible suffering that makes me grateful for what I have and less inclined to focus on what I may lack. I have seen orphaned children with crippling diseases. Young women forced into sexual slavery. Men imprisoned because they were too poor to pay a debt.

Suffering is universal and often unbelievably cruel, but even in the worst of slums and after the most horrible tragedies, I have been heartened to see people not only surviving but thriving. Joy was certainly not what I expected to find in a place called "Garbage City," the worst slum at the edge of Cairo, Egypt. The Manshiet Nasser neighborhood is tucked into towering rock cliffs. The unfortunate but accurate nickname and the community's rank odor come from the fact that most of its fifty thousand residents sustain themselves by combing through Cairo, dragging its garbage there, and picking through it. Each day they sort through mountains of refuse pulled from a city of eighteen million residents, hoping to find objects to sell, recycle, or somehow make use of.

Amid streets lined with garbage piles, pig pens, and stinking trash, you would expect people to be overcome with despair, yet I found it to be quite the opposite on a visit in 2009. The people there live hard lives, to be sure, but those I met were very caring, seemingly happy, and filled with faith. Egypt is 90 percent Muslim. Garbage City is the only predominantly Christian neighborhood. Nearly 98 percent of the people are Coptic Christians.

I've been to many of the poorest slums in all corners of the world. This was one of the worst as far as the environment, but it was also one of the most heart-warming in spirit. We squeezed nearly 150 people into a very small concrete building that served as their church. As I began speaking, I was struck by the joy and happiness radiating from my audience. They were simply beaming at me. My life has rarely seemed so blessed. I gave thanks that their faith lifted them above their circumstances as I told them how Jesus had changed my life too.

I spoke with church leaders there about how lives in the village had changed through the power of God. Their hope wasn't put on this earth, but their hope is in eternity. In the meantime they'll believe in miracles and thank God for who He is and what He has done. Before we left, we presented some families with rice, tea, and a small amount of cash that would buy them enough food for several weeks. We also distributed sports equipment, soccer balls, and jump ropes to the children. They immediately invited our group to play with them, and we had a ball, laughing and enjoying each other even though we were surrounded by squalor. I will never forget those children and their smiles. It just proved to me again that happiness can come to us under any circumstance if we put our total trust in God.

How can such impoverished children laugh? How can prisoners sing with joy? They rise above by accepting that certain events are beyond their control and beyond their understanding too, and then focusing instead on what they *can* understand and control. My parents did just that. They moved forward by deciding to trust in God's Word that "all things work for the good of those who love God, who are called according to His purpose."

A FAMILY OF FAITH

My mum and dad were both born into strong Christian families in the part of the former Yugoslavia now known as Serbia. Their families immigrated separately to Australia while they were young because of Communist repression. Their parents were Apostolic Christians, and their faith included conscientious objection to bearing arms. The Communists discriminated against them and persecuted them for their beliefs. They had to hold services in secret. They suffered financially because they refused to join the Communist Party, which controlled every aspect of life. When my father was young, he often went hungry for that reason.

Both sets of my grandparents joined many thousands of Serbian Christians who immigrated to Australia and also to the United States and Canada after World War II. My parents' families moved to Australia, where they and their children could be free to practice their Christian beliefs. Other members of their families moved to the United States and Canada around the same time, so I have many relatives in those countries too.

My parents met in a Melbourne church. My mum, Dushka, was in her second year of nursing school at the Royal Children's Hospital in Victoria. My dad, Boris, worked in office administration and cost accounting. He later became a lay pastor in addition to his job. When I was about seven years old, my parents began considering a move to the United States because they felt there might be better access to new prosthetics and medical care to help us deal with my disabilities.

My uncle Batta Vujicic had a construction and property management business in Agoura Hills just 35 miles outside Los Angeles. Batta always told my father he'd give him a job if he could obtain a work visa. There was a large community of Serbian Christians with several churches around Los Angeles, which also appealed to my parents. My father learned that obtaining a work visa was a long, drawn-out process. He decided to apply, but in the meantime my family moved a thousand miles north to Brisbane, Queensland, where the climate was better for me, as I had allergies along with my other challenges.

I was approaching ten years old and in my fourth year of elementary school when everything finally fell into place for a move to the United States. My parents felt that my younger siblings—my brother Aaron and sister Michelle—and I were at a good age for assimilating into the United States school system. We waited in Queensland for over eighteen months for Dad's three-year work visa to be arranged, finally moving in 1994.

Unfortunately, the move to California did not work out for several reasons. When we left Australia, I had already started sixth grade. My new school in Agoura Hills was very crowded. They could only get me into advanced classes, which was difficult enough, but in addition the curriculums were very different. I'd always been a good student, but I struggled to adapt to the change. Due to different school calendars, I was literally behind before I even started my classes in California. I had a difficult time catching up. The junior high I attended also required students to change classrooms for each subject, which was unlike Australia and added to the challenges of my adjustment.

We'd moved in with my uncle Batta, his wife Rita, and their six children, which made for a pretty crowded house even though they had a large home in Agoura Hills. We had planned to move into our own home as soon as possible, but home prices were much higher than in Australia. My father worked for Batta's real estate management company. My mother did not continue her nursing career because her first priority was to get us settled into our new schools and environment, and so she had not applied to become licensed to practice nursing in California.

After three months of living with Uncle Batta's family, my parents concluded that the move to the United States just wasn't working out. I was struggling in school, and my parents had difficulty arranging for my health insurance and overall handling the high cost of living in California. There were also concerns that we might never be able to secure permanent residency in the United States. A lawyer advised my family that my health challenges might make it more difficult to win approval because of possible doubts about my family's ability to keep up with medical costs and other expenses related to my disabilities.

With so many factors weighing on them, my parents decided to move back to Brisbane after only four months in the United States. They actually found a house in the same cul-de-sac where we'd lived before the move, so all of us kids could return to our same schools and friends. My dad went back to teaching computing and management in the College of Technical and Further Education. My mum devoted her life to my brother and sister and, mostly, me.

A CHALLENGING CHILD

In recent years my parents have been candid in describing their fears and nightmares immediately following my birth. As I was growing up, of course, they did not let on that I was not exactly the child of their dreams. In the months following my arrival, my mum feared she could not look after me. My dad could not see a happy future for me and worried about the kind of life I would have. If I was helpless and unable to experience life, he felt I would be better off with God. They considered their options, including the possibility of giving me up for adoption. Both sets of my grandparents offered to take me and care for me. My parents declined the offers. They decided it was their responsibility to raise me as best they could.

They grieved, and then they set about raising their physically challenged son to be as "normal" as he could possibly be. My parents are people of strong faith, and they kept thinking that God must have had some reason for giving them such a son.

Some injuries heal more quickly if you keep moving. The same is true of setbacks in life. Perhaps you lose your job. A relationship might not work out. Maybe the bills are piling up. Don't put your life on hold so that you can dwell on the unfairness of past hurts. Look instead for ways to move forward. Maybe there is a better job awaiting you that will be more fulfilling and rewarding. Your relationship may have needed a shake-up, or maybe there is someone better for you. Perhaps your financial challenges will inspire you to find new creative ways to save and build wealth.

You can't always control what happens to you. There are some occurrences in life that are not your fault or within your power to stop. The choice you have is either to give up or to keep on striving for a better life. My advice is to know that everything happens for a reason and in the end good will come of it.

As a child, I just assumed I was a perfectly adorable baby, naturally charming and as lovable as any on earth. My blissful ignorance was a blessing at that age. I didn't know that I was different or that many challenges awaited me. You see, I don't think we are ever given more than we can handle. I promise you that for every *disability* you have, you are blessed with more than enough *abilities* to overcome your challenges.

God equipped me with an amazing amount of determination and other gifts too. I soon proved that even without limbs I was athletic and well coordinated. I was all trunk but all baby boy too; a rolling, diving daredevil. I learned to haul myself into an upright position by bracing my forehead against a wall and scooting up it. My mum and dad worked with me for a long time trying to help me master a more comfortable method, but I always insisted on finding my own way.

My mum tried to help by putting cushions on the floor so I could use them to brace myself and get up, but for some reason I decided it was better just to bash my brow against the wall and inch my way up. Doing tasks my way, even if it was the hard way became my trademark!

Using my head was my only option in those early days; a fact that developed my massive intellect (kidding!) while also giving me the neck strength of a Brahma bull and a forehead hard as a bullet. My parents worried about me constantly, of course. Parenthood is a shocking experience even with full-bodied babies. New mothers and fathers often joke that they wish their first child came with an operating manual. There was no chapter even in Dr. Spock for babies like me. Yet I stubbornly grew healthier and bolder. I closed in on the "terrible twos" stage, packing more potential parental terrors than a set of octuplets.

How will he ever feed himself? How will he go to school? Who would take care of him if something happened to us? How will he ever live independently?

Our human powers of reasoning can be a blessing and a curse. Like my parents, you have probably fretted and worried about the future. Often, though, that which you dread turns out to be far less a problem than you imagined. There is nothing wrong with looking ahead and planning for the future, but know that your worst fears could just as easily prove to be your best surprise. Very often life works out for the good.

One of the best surprises of my childhood was the control I had over my little left foot. Instinctively I used it to roll myself around, to kick, shove, and brace myself. My parents and doctors felt that the handy little foot might be of greater use. There were two toes, but they were fused together when I was born. My parents and doctors decided that an operation to free the toes might allow me to use them more like fingers to grip a pen, turn a page, or perform other functions.

We then lived in Melbourne, Australia, which offered some of the best medical care in the country. I did present challenges beyond the training of most health care professionals. At the time when doctors were preparing me for foot surgery, my mum kept emphasizing to them that I ran hot most of the time and that they would have to be especially attentive to the possibility of my body overheating. She knew about another child without limbs who overheated during an operation and was left with brain damage after suffering a brain seizure.

My self-roasting tendencies prompted an oft-repeated family saying: "When Nicky's cold, the ducks must be freezing." Still, it is no joke that if I exercise too much, get stressed out, or stay too long under hot lights, my body temperature will rise dangerously. Avoiding a meltdown is one of the things I have to always be on guard against.

"Please monitor his temperature carefully," my mum told the surgical team. Even though the doctors knew my mother was a nurse, they still didn't take her advice seriously. They managed a successful surgery separating my toes, but what my mum had warned them about came to pass. I emerged from the operating room soaked because they hadn't taken any precautions for keeping my body from overheating, and when they realized that my temperature was getting out of control, they tried to cool me with wet sheets. They also put buckets of ice on me to avoid a seizure.

My mum was furious. No doubt the doctors felt the wrath of Dushka!

Even still, once I chilled out (quite literally), my quality of life received a big boost from my newly freed toes. They didn't work exactly as the doctors had hoped, but I adapted. It's amazing what a little foot and a couple of toes can do for a bloke with no arms and no legs. That operation and new technologies liberated me by giving me the power to operate custom-built electronic wheelchairs, a computer, and a cell phone too.

———

I can't know exactly what your burden is, nor do I pretend that I've ever been through a similar crisis, but look at what my parents went through when I was born. Imagine how they felt. Consider how bleak the future must have looked to them.

You may not be able to see a bright light at the end of your own dark tunnel right now, but know that my parents could not envision what a wonderful life I would have one day. They had no idea that their son would be not only self-sufficient and fully engaged in a career but happy, and full of joyful purpose!

Most of my parents' worst fears never materialized. Raising me was certainly not easy, but I think they'll tell you that for all the challenges, we had plenty of laughter and joy. All things considered, I had an amazingly normal childhood in which I enjoyed tormenting my siblings, Aaron and Michelle, just like all big brothers!

Life may be kicking you around right now. You may wonder if your fortunes will improve. I'm telling you that you can't even imagine the good that awaits you if you refuse to give up. Stay focused on your dream. Do whatever it takes to stay in the chase. You have the power to change your circumstances. Go after whatever it is you desire.

My life is an adventure still being written—and so is yours. Start writing the first chapter now! Fill it with adventure and love and happiness. Live the story as you write it!

SEARCHING FOR MEANING

I'll concede that for a long time I did not believe that I had any power over how my own story would turn out. I struggled to understand what difference I could make in the world or what path I should take. I was convinced while growing up that there was nothing good about my abbreviated body. Sure, I never had to get up from the dinner table because I hadn't washed my hands, and yes, I'd never known the pain of a stubbed toe, but these few benefits didn't seem like much consolation.

My brother and sister and my crazy cousins never let me feel sorry for myself. They never coddled me. They accept me for who I am, yet they also toughened me up with their teasing and pranks so that I could find humor instead of bitterness in my circumstances.

"Look at that kid in the wheelchair! He's an alien," my cousins would scream across the shopping mall, pointing at me. We all laughed hysterically at the reactions from strangers who had no idea that the kids picking on the disabled boy were really his strongest allies.

The older I become, the more I realize what a powerful gift it is to be loved like that. Even if at times you feel alone, you should know that *you* are loved too and recognize that God created you out of love. Therefore you are never alone. His love for you is unconditional. He doesn't love you *if* . . . He loves you always. Remind yourself of that when feelings of loneliness and despair come over you. Remember, those are just feelings. They are not real, but God's love is so real that He created you to prove it.

It is important to hold His love in your heart because there will be times when you feel vulnerable. My big family couldn't always be there to protect me. Once I went off to school, there was no hiding that I was so very different from everyone else. My dad assured me that God didn't make mistakes, but at times I couldn't shake the feeling that I was the exception to that rule.

"Why couldn't You give me just one arm?" I'd ask God. "Think what I could do with one arm!"

I'm sure you've had similar moments when you've prayed or simply wished for a dramatic change in your life. There is no reason to panic if your miracle doesn't arrive, or if your wish doesn't come true right this minute. Remember, God helps those who help themselves. It's still up to you to keep striving to serve the highest purpose for your talents and your dreams in the world around you.

For the longest time I thought that if my body were more "normal," my life would be a breeze. What I didn't realize was that I didn't have to be normal—I just had to be me, my father's child, carrying out God's plan. At first I was not willing to confront that what was really wrong with me wasn't my body, it was the limits I put on myself and my limited vision of the possibilities for my life.

If you aren't where you want to be or you haven't achieved all you hope to achieve, the reason most likely resides not around you but within you. Take responsibility and then take action. First, though, you must believe in yourself and your value. You can't wait for others to discover your hiding place. You can't wait for that miracle or "just the right opportunity." You should consider yourself the stick and the world your pot of stew. Stir it up.

As a boy, I spent many nights praying for limbs. I'd go to sleep crying and dream that I'd wake up to find they had miraculously appeared. It never happened, of course. Because I did not accept myself, I went off to school the next day and as a result found that acceptance from others was hard to come by.

Like most kids, I was more vulnerable in my pre-teen years, that time when everyone is trying to figure out where they fit in, who they are, and what the future holds. Often those who hurt me didn't set out to be cruel; they were just being typically blunt kids.

"Why don't you have arms and legs?" they'd ask.

My desire to fit in was the same as for any of my classmates. On my good days I won them over with my wit, my willingness to poke fun at myself, and by throwing my body around on the playground. On my worst days I hid behind the shrubbery or in empty classrooms to avoid being hurt or mocked. Part of the problem was that I'd spent more time with adults and older cousins than with kids my own age. I had a more mature outlook, and my more serious thoughts sometimes took me into dark places.

I'll never get a girl to love me. I don't even have arms to hold a girlfriend. If I have children, I'll never be able to hold them either. What sort of job could I ever have? Who would hire me? For most jobs, they'd have to hire a second person just to help me do what I was supposed to do. Who would ever hire one for the price of two?

My challenges were mostly physical, but clearly they affected me emotionally as well. I went through a very scary period of depression at a young age. Then, to my everlasting shock and gratitude, as

I moved into my teen years, I gradually won acceptance, first from myself and then from others.

Everyone goes through times when they feel excluded, alienated, or unloved. We all have our insecurities. Most kids fear they'll be mocked because their noses are too big or their hair is too curly. Adults fear that they won't be able to pay the bills or that they will fail to live up to expectations.

You will face moments of doubt and fear. We all do. Feeling down is natural; it is part of being perfectly human. Such feelings pose a danger only if you allow negative thoughts to stick around instead of just letting them wash over you.

When you trust that you have blessings—talents, knowledge, love—to share with others, you will begin the journey to self acceptance even if your gifts are not yet apparent. Once you begin that walk, others will find you and walk with you.

SPEAKING UP

I found the path to my purpose while trying to reach out to my classmates. If you've ever had to be the new kid in the corner, eating lunch all by yourself, I'm sure you understand that being the new kid in the corner in a wheelchair could be all the more difficult. Our moves from Melbourne to Brisbane, to the United States, and back to Brisbane forced me to make adjustments that added to my challenges.

My new classmates often assumed I was mentally as well as physically disabled. They usually kept their distance unless I summoned the courage to strike up conversations in the lunchroom or in the hallway. The more I did this, the more they accepted that I really wasn't an alien dropped into their midst.

Sometimes, you see, God expects you to help out with the heavy lifting. You can wish. You can dream. You can hope. But you must also act upon those wishes, those dreams, and those hopes. You have to stretch beyond where you are to reach where you want to be. I wanted people at my school to know that I was just like them on the inside, but I had to go outside my comfort zone to do that. Reaching out to them in this way brought out awesome rewards.

In time these discussions with classmates about coping in a world made for arms and legs led to invitations for me to speak to student groups, church youth groups, and other teen organizations. There's a wonderful truth that's so central to living. I find it extraordinary that schools do not teach it. The essential truth is this: Each of us has some gift—a talent, a skill, a craft, a knack—that gives us pleasure and engages us, and the path to our happiness often lies within that gift.

If you are still searching, still trying to figure out where you fit in and what fulfills you, I suggest you do a self-assessment. Sit down with a pen and paper or at a computer and make a list of your favorite activities. What do you find yourself drawn to do? What can you spend hours doing, losing track of time and place, and still want to do it again and again? Now, what is it that other people see in you? Do they compliment your talent for organization or your analytical skills? If you're not really sure what others see in you, ask your family and friends what they think you are best at.

These are the clues to finding your life's path, a path that lies secreted within you. We all arrive on this earth naked and full of promise. We come packed with presents waiting to be opened. When you find something that so fully engages you that you would do it for free all day every day, then you are on course. When you find someone who is willing to pay you for it, then you have a career.

At first my informal little talks to other young people were a way to reach out to them, to show that I was just like them. I was focused inward, grateful for a chance to share my world and to make connections. I knew what speaking did for me, but it took a while to realize that what I had to say might have an impact on others.

FINDING A PATH

One day I gave a talk to a group of about three hundred teenage students, probably the biggest group I'd ever addressed. I was sharing my feelings and my faith when something wonderful happened. Now and then students or teachers would shed tears when I told them about challenges I'd faced, but during this particular talk a girl in the audience completely broke down sobbing. I wasn't sure what had happened—perhaps I'd triggered some terrible memory for her. I was amazed when she then summoned the courage to raise her hand to speak, despite her sadness and tears. Bravely, she asked if she could come forward and give me a hug. Wow! I was floored.

I invited her up, and she wiped away her tears as she walked to the front of the room. She then gave me this huge hug, one of the best of my life. By then nearly everyone in the room was teary-eyed, including me. But I lost it entirely when she whispered in my ear:

"Nobody has ever told me that I'm beautiful the way that I am. No one has ever said that they love me," she said. "You've changed my life, and you are a beautiful person too."

Up to that point, I was still constantly questioning my own worth. I'd thought of myself as someone who simply gave little talks as a way of reaching out to other teens. First of all she called me "beautiful" (which didn't hurt), but more than anything she gave me that first real inkling that my speaking could help others. This girl changed my perspective. *Maybe I really do have something to contribute*, I thought.

Experiences like that helped me realize that being "different" just might help me contribute something special to the world. I found that people were willing to listen to me speak because they had only to look at me to know I'd faced and overcome my challenges. I did not lack credibility. Instinctively, people felt I might have something to say that could help them with their own problems.

God has used me to reach people in countless schools, churches, prisons, orphanages, hospitals, stadiums, and meeting halls. Even better, I've hugged thousands of people in face-to-face encounters that allow me to tell them how very precious they are. It's also my pleasure to assure them that He does have a plan for their lives. God took my unusual body and invested me with the ability to uplift hearts and encourage spirits, just as He says in the Bible: "For I know the plans I have for you . . . plans to prosper you and not to harm you, plans to give you hope and a future."

MAKING IT HAPPEN

Life can seem cruel, no doubt about it. Sometimes the bad breaks pile up and you just can't see a way out. You may not like the sound of that, but maybe you still aren't convinced that it can happen for you right now.

The fact is that as mere mortals, you and I have limited vision. We can't possibly see what lies ahead. That's both the bad news and the good news. My encouragement to you is that what lies ahead may be far better than anything you ever thought possible. But it's up to you to get over it, get up, and show up!

Whether your life is good and you want to make it better, or whether it's so bad you just want to stay in bed, the fact is that what happens from this very moment is up to you and your Maker. True, you can't control everything. Too often bad stuff happens to people no matter how good they are. It may not be fair that you weren't born into a life of ease, but if that is your reality, you have to work with it.

You may stumble. Others may doubt you. When I focused on

public speaking as a career path, even my parents questioned my decision.

"Don't you think that an accounting career, with your own practice, would be more appropriate for your circumstances and provide a better future?" my dad asked.

Yes, from most perspectives a career in accounting probably made more sense for me because I do have a talent for number-crunching. But from an early age I've had this absolute passion for sharing my faith and my hope of a better life. When you find your true purpose, passion follows. You absolutely live to pursue it.

If you are still searching for your path in life, know that it's okay to feel a little frustration. This is a marathon, not a sprint. Your yearning for more meaning is a sign that you are growing, moving beyond limitations, and developing your talents. It's healthy to look at where you are from time to time and to consider whether your actions and priorities are serving your highest purpose.

LIGHTING THE WAY

At fifteen years old I made my life right with God, asking Him for forgiveness and for direction. I asked Him to light my path of purpose. After being baptized four years later, I began speaking about my faith to others and knew I had found my calling. My career as a speaker and evangelist grew into a global ministry, and just a few years ago, quite unexpectedly, something happened that lifted my heart even higher and confirmed for me that I'd chosen the right path.

Nothing felt out of the ordinary on that Sunday morning when I rolled into a California church for a speaking engagement. Unlike most of my appearances, which happened in far-off corners of the world, this one was close to home. The Knott Avenue Christian Church in Anaheim is just down the road from my house.

As I entered in my wheelchair, the choir was beginning its opening song, and the service was starting. I took a seat on a bench at the front as the congregation filled the large church, and I began to mentally prepare for my speech. This would be my first time talking to the people at Knott Avenue, and I didn't expect they knew much about me, so I was surprised to hear someone calling, "Nick! Nick!" over the singing voices.

I didn't recognize the voice and was not even sure that I was the "Nick" being summoned. But when I turned around, I saw an older gentleman waving directly at me.

"Nick! Over here!" he shouted again.

Now that he had my attention, he pointed to a younger man standing next to him in the packed church who appeared to be holding a child. There were so many people crowded together that at first I could see only a flash of the toddler's bright eyes, a thatch of shiny brown hair, and a big gap-toothed baby smile.

Then the man held the little boy higher above the crowd so I could see him more clearly. The full view sent a wave of feeling through me so intense that (if I'd had them) it would have made my knees buckle.

The bright-eyed boy was just like me. No arms. No legs. He even had a little left foot like mine. Though he was only nineteen months old, he was *exactly* like me. I understood why the two men were so eager for me to see him. As I later learned, this boy's name is Daniel Martinez, the son of Chris and Patty.

I was supposed to be preparing for my speech, but seeing Daniel—seeing myself in that child—triggered such a swirl of feelings that I couldn't think straight. I first felt compassion for him and his family. But then sharp memories and anguished emotions bombarded me as I was vividly brought back to how I had felt at about that age, and I realized that he must have been going through the same things.

I know how he feels, I thought. *I've already been through what he will experience.* Looking at Daniel, I felt this incredible connection and a surge of empathy for him. Old feelings of insecurity, frustration, and loneliness flooded back, pulling the air out of my lungs. I felt like I was baking under the stage lights. I felt woozy. It wasn't a panic attack exactly; the vision of this boy in front of me touched the boy inside me.

Then I had a revelation that brought a sense of calm. *When I was growing up, I had no one who shared my situation who could help guide me, but now Daniel has someone. I can help him. My parents can help his parents. He doesn't have to go through what I went through. Perhaps I can spare him some of the pain that I had to endure.* Here I could clearly see that as difficult as it might be to live without limbs, my life still had value to be shared. There was nothing I lacked that would prevent me from making a difference in the world. My joy would be to encourage and inspire others. Even if I didn't change this planet as much as I would like, I'd still know with certainty that my life was not wasted. I was and am determined to make a contribution. You should believe in your power to do the same.

Life without meaning has no hope. Life without hope has no faith. If you find a way to contribute, you will find your meaning, and hope and faith will naturally follow and accompany you into your future.

My visit to the Knott Avenue church was intended to inspire and encourage others. Though seeing a boy so much like me floating over the crowd initially threw me off, he was a powerful confirmation of the difference I could make in the lives of many people, especially those facing major challenges, such as Daniel and his parents.

This encounter was so compelling that I had to share what I was seeing and feeling with the congregation, so I invited Daniel's parents to bring him up to the podium.

"There are no coincidences in life," I said. "Every breath, every step is ordained by God. It was no coincidence that another boy with no arms and no legs is in this room."

As I said that, Daniel flashed a radiant smile, captivating everyone in the church. The congregation fell silent as his father held him upright and alongside me. The sight of us together, a young man and an infant with shared challenges, beaming at each other, set off weeping and sniffling in the pews around us.

I don't cry easily, but as everyone around me unleashed a flood of tears, I couldn't help but get swept up too. At home that night, I remember saying not a single word. I kept thinking of this child and how he must be feeling just what I'd felt at his age. I thought also of how he would feel as his awareness grew, as he encountered the cruelties and rejection I'd experienced. I was sad for him and the suffering he likely would endure, but then I was heartened because I knew my parents and I could ease his burden and even light hope in his heart. I couldn't wait to tell my parents because I knew they would be eager to meet this boy and to give him and his parents hope. My mum and dad had been through so much and they'd had no one to guide them. I knew they would be grateful for the opportunity to help this family.

MOMENT OF MEANING

It had been a surreal, awestruck moment for me. I had been speechless (a rarity), and when Daniel looked up at me, my heart had melted. I still thought of myself as a kid, and having never seen anybody else like me, I badly wanted to know I wasn't alone, that I wasn't different from every single person on the planet. I felt that no one really understood what I was going through or could comprehend my pain or my loneliness.

Reflecting on my childhood, I was struck by all the pain I'd gone through just by being aware of how different I was. When others mocked or shunned me, it heightened the hurt all the more. But compared to the infinite mercy and glory and power of God I was now feeling because of this moment with Daniel, my pain was suddenly insignificant.

I would not wish my disability on anyone, so I was sad for Daniel. Yet I knew God had brought this child to me so that I could ease his burden. It was as if God were winking at me and saying, *Got you! See, I did have a plan for you!*

TAKE HEART

Of course I don't have all the answers. I don't know the specific pain or challenges you face. I came into this world shortchanged physically, but I've never known the pain of abuse or neglect. I've never had to deal with a broken family. I've never lost a parent or a brother or a sister. There are many bad experiences I've been spared. I'm certain that I've had it easier in thousands of ways than many people.

In that life-changing moment when I looked out and saw Daniel held above the crowd in that church, I realized that I'd become the miracle that I'd prayed for. God had not given me such a miracle. But he had made me Daniel's instead.

I was twenty-four years old when I met Daniel. When his mother, Patty, hugged me later that day, she said it was like stepping into the future and hugging her own grown-up son.

"You have no idea. I've been praying that God would send me a sign to let me know that He has not forgotten my son or me," she said. "You are a miracle. You are *our* miracle."

One of the great aspects of our meeting was that on that Sunday my parents were on their way from Australia for their first visit since I'd moved to the United States a year before. A couple days later my mum and dad met with Daniel and his parents. You can believe that they had a lot to talk about.

Chris and Patty may have considered me a blessing for Daniel, but my parents were an even bigger blessing to them. Who better to prepare them and guide them through the parenting of a child without arms and legs? We could give them not just hope but solid evidence that Daniel could live a fairly normal life, and that he too would discover the blessings he was meant to share. We have been blessed to share our experiences with them, to encourage them and to offer proof that there are no limits to a life without limbs.

At the same time Daniel is a dynamo who is a blessing to me, giving me far more than I could ever give him because of his energy and joy, and that is another, totally unexpected reward.

A LIFE TO SHARE

The late Helen Keller lost her sight and hearing before the age of two due to illness, but she went on to become a world-renowned author, speaker, and social activist. This great woman said true happiness comes through "fidelity to a worthy purpose."

What does that mean? For me, it means being faithful to your gifts, growing them, sharing them, and taking joy in them. It means moving beyond the pursuit of self-satisfaction to the more mature search for meaning and fulfillment.

The greatest rewards come when you give of yourself. It's about bettering the lives of others, being part of something bigger than yourself, and making a positive difference. You don't have to be Mother Teresa to do that. You can even be a "disabled" guy and make an impact. Just ask the young lady who sent this e-mail to our Life Without Limbs Web site.

Dear Nick,

Wow, I don't even know where to begin. I guess I will start off by introducing myself. I am 16 years old. I am writing to you because I watched your DVD "No Arms, No Legs,

No Worries," and it made the biggest impact on my life and my recovery. I say recovery because I am recovering from an eating disorder, anorexia. I have been in and out of inpatient treatment centers for the past year now, and it has been the worst chapter of my life so far. I was recently discharged from a residential treatment center located in California. While I was there, I saw your DVD. I have never felt so inspired and motivated in my entire life. You truly amaze me. Everything about you is so wonderful and so positive. Every single word that came out of your mouth made some sort of an impact on me. I have never been so incredibly grateful in my life. I mean there have been times in my life when I thought I had reached the end, but now I see that everyone does have a purpose in life, and that they should respect themselves for who they are. Wow, seriously—I can't even thank you enough for all the encouragement your DVD gave me. I wish that one day I can meet you; it's something I dream to do before I die. You have the best personality a human being could have—you made me laugh so much (which is very hard to do when in rehab). Because of you I am now a lot stronger and more aware of who I am and I no longer obsess about what other people think of me, or put myself down all the time. You taught me how to turn my negatives into positives. Thank you for saving my life and turning it around. I can't thank you enough—you are my hero!

USE ME UP

I am grateful to receive many letters like that, and it seems especially odd given how despondent I was as a child about ever enjoying my own life, much less helping others with theirs. Your search for meaning may still be under way. But I don't think you can really feel fulfilled without serving others. Each of us hopes to put our talents and knowledge to use for benefits beyond paying the bills.

In today's world, even though we may be fully conscious of the spiritual emptiness of material attainment, we still need reminders that fulfillment has nothing to do with having possessions. People certainly try the strangest options for attaining fulfillment. They may drink a six-pack of beer. They may drug themselves into oblivion. They may alter their bodies to achieve some arbitrary standard of beauty. They may work their whole lives to reach the pinnacle of success, only to have it mercilessly yanked from them in a second. But most sensible people know that there are no easy routes to long-term happiness. If you place your bets on temporary pleasures, you will find only temporary satisfaction. With cheap thrills, you get what you pay for—here today, gone tomorrow.

Life isn't about having, it's about being. You could surround yourself with all that money can buy, and you'd still be as miserable as a human can be. I know people with perfect bodies who don't have half the happiness I've found. On my journeys I've seen more joy in the slums of Mumbai and the orphanages of Africa than in wealthy gated communities and on sprawling estates worth millions.

Why is that?

You'll find contentment when your talents and passion are completely engaged, in full force. Recognize instant self-gratification for what it is. Resist the temptation to grab for material objects like the perfect house, the coolest clothes, or the hottest car. The *if I just had X, I would be happy* syndrome is a mass delusion. When you look for happiness in mere objects, they are never enough.

Look around. Look within.

————

As a boy, I figured that if God would just give me arms and legs, I would be happy for the rest of my life. It hardly seemed selfish since limbs are standard equipment. Still, as you know, I found that I can be happy and fulfilled without the usual appendages. Daniel helped confirm that for me. The experience of reaching out to him and his family reminded me why I am on this earth.

Once my parents arrived in California, we met with Daniel's family and I witnessed something so special. My parents and I spent hours talking to his mother and father, comparing experiences, discussing how we've dealt with challenges that await him. From those first days we formed a strong bond that remains to this day.

About a year after our first meeting, we got together again, and during our discussion Daniel's parents noted that his doctors felt he wasn't ready to have his own customized wheelchair like mine.

"Why not?" I asked. "I was about Daniel's age when I started driving my own wheelchair."

To prove my point, I hopped out of my chair and let Daniel take my seat. His foot fit the joystick perfectly. He loved it! He did a great job maneuvering the chair. Because we were there, Daniel had the opportunity to prove to his parents that he could handle a customized wheelchair. This was one of the many ways I knew I could be there for him and help light his path based on my shared experiences. I can't tell you what a thrill it is to serve as Daniel's guide.

We provided Daniel with a rare gift that day, but he presented me with an even better one in the matchless fulfillment I felt at feeling his joy. Not a luxury car. Not a McMansion. Nothing compares to fulfilling your destiny and aligning with His plan.

This gift just keeps on giving. In a later visit with Daniel and his family, my parents shared their early concerns that I could easily drown in the bathtub without arms and legs to keep me afloat. As a result they were very careful when bathing me as an infant, and as I grew older, my dad held me in the water gently, showing me that I could float. Over time I became more confident and adventurous and learned I could float easily as long as I held a bit of air in my lungs. I even figured out how to use my little foot as a propeller to motor myself through the water. Considering how frightened my parents had understandably been about me in the water, imagine their amazement as I became an avid swimmer, leaping into any pool of water I could find.

After sharing that story with Daniel's family, we were delighted to learn later that one of the first phrases he said to his parents when he was old enough to speak clearly was: "Swim like Nick!" Now Daniel too is an avid swimmer. I can't express to you how awesome that makes me feel. To see Daniel benefit from my experiences gives deeper meaning to my life. If my story never touched another person, Daniel's determination to "swim like Nick" would be enough to make my life and all the hardships I've encountered worthwhile.

Recognizing your purpose means everything. I assure you that you too have something to contribute. You may not see it now, but you would not be on this planet if that were not true. I know for certain that God does not make mistakes, but he does make miracles. I am one. You are too.

TWO

No Arms, No Legs, No Limits

Time and again in my life and in my travels, I have witnessed the incredible power of the human spirit. I know for certain that miracles happen, but only for those who hang on to hope. What is hope? It is where dreams begin. It is the voice of your purpose. It speaks to you and reassures you that whatever happens to you doesn't live within you. You may not control what happens to you, but you can control how you respond.

The late Reverend Martin Luther King, Jr., said, "Everything that is done in the world is done by hope." I know for certain that as long as you draw breath, hope is available to you. You and I are only human. We cannot see into the future. Instead, we picture the possibilities for what might be. Only God knows how our lives will unfold. Hope is His gift to us, a window to look through. We cannot know the future He has planned for us. Trust in Him, keep hope in your heart, and even when faced with the worst, do whatever you can to prepare yourself for the best!

Sometimes, of course, our prayers are not answered. Tragedies occur despite our prayers and our faith. Even the best people with the purest of hearts sometimes suffer horrible losses and grief. The recent deadly earthquakes in Haiti, Chile, Mexico, and China are just the most recent examples that tremendous suffering and tragedy occur every day. Thousands died in those natural catastrophes. Their hopes and dreams died with them. Many mothers lost their children. Many children lost their mothers.

How do you sustain hope amid such suffering? One thing that sustains me when I hear of these great calamities is the fact that they always trigger incredible caring from other human beings. Just when you wonder why, amid such senseless suffering, people would still have hope, hundreds of selfless volunteers pour into those regions. Students, doctors, engineers, and other rescuers and rebuilders give of themselves and their talents to help those who have survived.

Hope appears even in the worst of times to give us proof of God's presence. My own suffering seems so slight in comparison to the trials endured by so many people I've met, but I've also grieved the loss of a loved one. Our family lost my cousin Roy to cancer at the age of twenty-seven, despite the fervent prayers of all the devout Christians in our family, church, and community. Losing someone so close to you is heartbreaking and difficult to understand, which is why having hope is so important to me. You see, my hope extends beyond our worldly existence. The ultimate hope is in heaven. My family takes no little consolation in the hope that my cousin, who believed in Jesus Christ, is in heaven with Him and suffering no more.

Even in the worst situations that seem beyond our capacities, God knows how much our hearts can bear. I hold on to the belief that our life here is temporary, as we are being prepared for eternity. Whether our lives here are good or bad, the promise of heaven awaits. I always have hope in the most difficult times that God will give me the strength to endure the challenges and the heartache and that better days await, if not on this earth then for certain in heaven.

One of the best ways I've found for holding on even when our prayers are not answered is to reach out to others. If your suffering is a burden, reach out to ease that of someone else and bring hope to them. Lift them up so that they will be comforted with the knowledge that they are not alone in their suffering. Offer compassion when you need it. Be a friend when you need friendship. Give hope when you most need it.

I am young and I don't pretend to have all the answers, but more and more I realize that in those times when hopelessness seems to prevail, when our prayers go unanswered, and when our worst fears are realized, our salvation lies in our relationships with those around us and, especially for me and fellow Christians, in our relationship with God and our trust in His love and wisdom.

A POWERFUL GIFT

My belief in the power of hope over despair was reinforced on my first visit to China in 2008. I saw the Great Wall and marveled at the grandeur of one of the world's most incredible wonders. But the most powerful moment of this trip for me came when I saw the joyful glimmer in the eyes of a young Chinese girl. She was performing with other children who'd put together a show worthy of an Olympic spectacle. This girl's jubilant expression caught my attention, and I could not look away. While she moved in precision with the other dancers, she simultaneously balanced a spinning plate overhead. She was concentrating so, so hard, yet despite everything she had to think about, she still had this look of intense happiness that moved me to tears.

You see, this girl and all the children in the show were among more than four thousand young people orphaned by a massive earthquake that had hit the region just a few months earlier. My caregiver, our travel coordinator, and I had come to this orphanage with supplies for them, and I'd been asked to speak to them to raise their spirits.

As we traveled to the orphanage, I was overwhelmed by the damage and suffering that had been caused by the earthquake. In the face of such devastation I worried that I would not know what to tell these orphans. The earth had opened up and swallowed everything they'd loved and known. I had never endured anything so terrible. What could I say to them? We'd brought warm coats and other clothing for them, but how could I give them hope?

When I arrived at the orphanage, I was mobbed. One child after another embraced me. I didn't speak their language, but it didn't matter. Their faces said it all. Despite their circumstances, they were radiant. I should not have worried about what words to say to help them. I didn't have to inspire these children. Instead, they inspired me with the soaring spirit of their performance that day. They'd lost their parents, their homes, and all their belongings, yet they were expressing joy.

I told them I admired their courageous spirits and urged them to keep looking forward, to dare to wish for better lives, and to pursue their dreams with all their power.

DARE TO DREAM

Have the courage to pursue your own dreams, and never doubt your ability to meet whatever challenges come your way. I've seen people's amazing capacity to rise above their circumstances not only in Chinese orphanages but in the slums of Mumbai and the prisons of Romania. I recently spoke at a social welfare center in South Korea, where some of the residents were disabled and others were single mothers. The power of their spirits amazed me. I visited a prison in South Africa with concrete walls and rusted bars. The worst criminals were not allowed in our chapel service, but I could hear others outside, throughout the prison, singing along to the gospel music. It was as if the Holy Spirit had filled the entire population with God's joy. They were captive on the outside but free on the inside because of their faith and their hope. Walking out of the prison gates that day, I felt that those inmates seemed freer than many of those outside the prison gates. You too can allow hope to live in your heart.

Remember that sadness does serve a purpose. It is perfectly natural to experience this emotion, but you should never let it dominate your thoughts day and night. You can control your response by turning to more positive thoughts and actions that lift your spirits.

Because I am a spiritual person, I look to my faith in sorrowful times. But (perhaps surprisingly) it is my training in accounting that offers a more pragmatic approach. If you say you are without hope, that means you think there is *zero* chance of anything good happening in your life ever again.

Zero? That's pretty extreme, don't you think? The power of believing in better days is so indisputable that, to me, it seems far more probable that your days will change for the better. Hope, along with faith and love, is one of the pillars of spirituality. Whatever your beliefs, you should never be without it because everything good in life begins with it. If you didn't have hope, would you ever plan to start a family? Without hope, would you ever try to learn something new? Hope is the springboard for nearly every step we take, and my hope in writing this book is that you will find a better life, one without limits.

A passage in the Bible says, "Those who hope in the Lord will renew their strength. They will soar on wings like eagles; they will run and not grow weary, they will walk and not be faint." The first time I heard this passage, I realized that I didn't need arms and legs. Don't ever forget that God never gives up on you. Keep moving ahead because action creates momentum, which in turn creates unanticipated opportunities.

RIPPLES BECOME TIDES

People around the world were deeply saddened by the devastating 2009 earthquake in Haiti. Yet for all the tragedies that came with this massive disaster, the horrific circumstances also brought out people's best qualities, as in the survivors who refused to surrender despite the overwhelming odds stacked against them.

Marie's son Emmanuel was believed to be among the dead buried under a building. The twenty-one-year-old tailor had been with his mother in her apartment when the earthquake hit. She escaped, but she could not find him afterward, their building now just a heap of rubble. Marie looked for her son at an emergency camp set up for people who'd lost their homes, but she could not find him among the other survivors. She waited, hoping he still might make his way there.

After several days, she went back through the chaos and the destruction to search for her son. Heavy machinery at work on the site made it difficult to hear, but at one point Marie thought she heard Emmanuel calling for her.

"At that moment," she told a reporter, "I knew it was possible to save him."

Marie let everyone know that her son had called to her from under the rubble, but no one was able to help her. But when international groups of rescue workers arrived, she was able to find an experienced team of engineers. She convinced them that her son was still alive. Using their equipment and knowledge, they cut through steel, concrete, and debris at exactly the spot where she'd heard her son's voice.

They kept digging until they uncovered Emmanuel's hand. He was reaching out to them. They continued until they freed his shoulder and they were able to pull him out. He had been buried for ten days. He was severely dehydrated, covered in dust, and very hungry, but he survived.

Sometimes all you will have is your belief that anything is possible, that miracles can happen. As it was for Marie, the world around you may be in chaos, but you should not give in to despair. Instead, believe that whatever you lack, God will provide! That belief spurred Marie to action. Her actions brought her within reach of her son's voice. It's not a stretch to recognize that Marie's hope kept Emmanuel alive, is it?

Life may not be going well for you now, but as long as you are here, as long as you press forward, *anything* is possible.

LIVE WITH HOPE IN YOUR HEART

You may be skeptical that anything is possible by hanging on to hope. Or perhaps you have been brought down so low that finding the strength to crawl out of your despair seems impossible. There was a time when I felt exactly that way. I was absolutely convinced that my life would never be of value and that I would only be a burden to those I loved.

My parents were not prepared for a child without limbs when I was born, and as a result they were despondent. Who could blame them? Every mother and father tries to envision the future for the children they bring into the world. My parents had difficulty projecting what sort of future I would have, and as I grew older, so did I.

We all have at times seen our vision for our lives crash into a cruel reality like a speeding car into a brick wall. The particulars of your experience may be unique, but situations of despair are all too human. Teens often e-mail me stories of abuse and neglect ripping apart their families. Adults share stories in which drugs or alcohol or pornography have left them crippled. Some days it seems like half the people I talk to are dealing with cancer or some other life-threatening medical condition.

How do you stay hopeful in such situations? You trust in God, remember that you are here for a reason, and dedicate yourself to fulfilling that purpose. Whatever challenge you are facing, you are blessed in ways that will help you find a way through it. Just think of my parents and of the hopelessness that they once faced.

BELIEVE IN THE BEST

Remaining positive and motivated when your burden feels unbearable is undoubtedly difficult. When I became old enough to understand the challenges awaiting me, I was often haunted by despair and couldn't begin to imagine that anything positive lay in store for me. My memories of the darkest days of my childhood are hazy. I was going through one of those periods when being different was particularly tough. I'm sure you have experienced those self-doubts too. We all want to fit in, but at times we all feel like outsiders.

My insecurities and doubts sprang mostly from the physical challenges of having no arms or legs. I cannot know what your concerns are, but hanging on to hope helped me. Here is just one, early experience of how it worked in my world:

I was just a toddler when my medical team recommended that my parents put me in a play group with other kids labeled "disabled." Their challenges ranged from missing limbs to cystic fibrosis and severe mental disorders. My parents had great love and empathy for other special needs kids and their families, but they don't think any child should be limited to one group of playmates. They held on to the conviction that my life would have no limits, and they fought to keep that dream alive.

My mother, bless her, made an important decision at an early stage of my life. "Nicholas, you need to play with normal children because you are normal. You just have a few bits and pieces missing, that's all," she said, setting the tone for years to come. She didn't want me to feel less than normal or restricted in any way.

She didn't want me to become introverted, shy, or insecure just because I was different physically.

Little did I realize that my parents were even then instilling in me the belief that I had every right to a life free of labels and restrictions. You have that right too. You should demand to be free of whatever categorizations or limits others try to put on you. Because of my missing bits and pieces, I am sensitive to the fact that some people accept what others say about them and even unconsciously restrict themselves. There certainly were times when I was tired or cranky and tried to claim that studying or going to the doctor was just too taxing, but my parents refused to let me hide behind that.

Labels can provide a tempting hiding place. Some people use them as excuses. Others rise above them. Many, many people have been labeled "handicapped" or "disabled," only to soar above, enjoying dynamic lives and doing important things. I encourage you to rise above any attempt to restrict you from exploring and developing your gifts.

As a child of God, I know that He is always with me, and I'm comforted to know that He understands how much we can bear. When others share stories with me of their own challenges and trials, I'm often moved to tears. I remind those who are suffering or grieving that God's arm is never too short. He can reach anyone.

Draw strength from that. Dare to give it a go and to soar as high as your imagination will take you. You can expect challenges. Welcome them as "character-building experiences." Learn from them and rise above them. You may have an excellent dream. Just be open-minded enough to accept that God may have a different path for you than the one you envisioned. There are many ways to reach your dream, so don't be discouraged if you can't yet see the way on your own.

BIONIC BOY

Hope is a catalyst. It can even move obstacles that seem immovable. When you keep pushing, refusing to give up, you create momentum. Hope creates opportunities you never would have anticipated. Helpful people are drawn to you. Doors open. Paths are cleared.

Remember—action brings reaction. When you are tempted to abandon your dreams, push yourself to continue one more day, one more week, one more month, and one more year. You will be amazed at what happens when you refuse to quit.

When it came time for me to begin elementary school, my parents again lobbied for me to have a typical education. As a result of their unyielding conviction, I became one of the first disabled children in Australia to "mainstream" into the regular school system. I did so well in the mainstream school that the local newspaper ran a story with the headline "Integration lets disabled boy blossom." The story, accompanied by a big photograph of my sister Michelle riding with me in my wheelchair, set off a national media blitz that brought visits from government officials, cards, letters, gifts, and invitations from across the country.

The donations that flowed in after that newspaper story helped fund my parents' efforts to equip me with replacement limbs. They'd been trying to fit me with artificial limbs since I was eighteen months old. My first prosthesis was just one arm, which didn't work well for me. The arm and hand were operated mechanically with pulleys and levers, and it weighed about twice as much as all the rest of me!

Just keeping my balance with this contraption on was a challenge. I managed to operate it after a while. I'd already become adept at grabbing objects with my little foot, my chin, or my teeth, so the bionic arm seemed only to make daily chores more difficult. My parents were disappointed at first, but my confidence grew because I felt good about doing so well on my own. I encouraged them and thanked them and looked ahead.

There is power in perseverance. Our first experiment with an artificial limb failed, but I continued to believe my life would work out for the best. My optimism and high spirits inspired our community Lions Club, an international service organization, to raise more than $200,000 for my medical bills and a new wheelchair. Some of those funds also helped us travel to Toronto, Canada, to try a more advanced set of electronic arms developed by a children's clinic. In the end, however, even the medical experts decided that I managed to accomplish most tasks more efficiently on my own without the aid of prosthetics.

I was excited that there were scientists and inventors intent on providing me with limbs someday. But I became all the more determined to do whatever I could without waiting for someone else to find something that would improve my life—I had to find my own answers. Even today I welcome anyone who helps me, whether it is opening a door for my wheelchair or giving me a drink from a glass of water. We need to take responsibility for our own happiness and success. Your friends and family may reach out to you in times of need. Be grateful for that. Welcome their efforts, but keep pushing on your own too. The more effort you put into it, the more opportunities you create.

Sometimes you may feel like you are just about to realize your goal only to fall short. That is no reason to quit. Defeat happens only to those who refuse to try again. I still believe that one day I will be able to walk and lift and hold utensils like a regular person. It will be a miracle when that happens, whether God does it on His own or through his agents on earth. The technology for robotic limbs is advancing rapidly. Someday I may be able to wear prosthetic arms and legs that work efficiently, but for now I'm happy to be just as I am.

Often the very challenges that we think are holding us back are, in fact, making us stronger. You should be open to the possibility that today's handicap might be tomorrow's advantage. I've come to see my lack of limbs as an asset. Men, women, and children who can't speak my language only have to see me to know that I have overcome many challenges. My lessons, they know, did not come easily.

WISDOM BORN OF EXPERIENCE

When I tell my audiences to hold on for better days, I speak from experience. You can believe and trust in what I say because I have been there. At one point in my life I gave up hope.

This low point in my mostly happy childhood came around the age of ten, when negative thoughts overwhelmed me. No matter how optimistic and determined and inventive I tried to be, there were some tasks I just could not do. Some of them were simple, everyday activities. It really bothered me, for example, that I couldn't grab a soda out of the refrigerator like every other kid. I couldn't feed myself, and I hated to ask other people to do it. I felt bad that they had to interrupt their meals to help me.

Other, bigger issues haunted me in this period of my life: *Would I ever find a wife to love me? How would I provide for her and our children? How could I protect them if they were threatened?*

Most people have such thoughts. You probably have wondered at some point whether you would ever have a lasting relationship, a secure job, or a safe place to live. It is normal and healthy to look ahead because that is how we develop a vision for our lives. The problem comes when negative thoughts block your vision for the future and cloud your mind. I pray and I remind myself of the word of God, who helps me know that He is with me. He never leaves me. He hasn't forgotten me. He will cause even the worst things to come together for the good. I remind myself to hold on to the promises of God, no matter what I see on the outside. I know that God is good. If He allows something bad to happen, I may not understand, but I can hold on to His goodness.

MONITOR YOUR THOUGHTS

As my eleventh birthday approached, I entered the tricky adolescent stage when our brains rewire and strange chemicals flow through out bodies. Other boys and girls my age were starting to pair up, which added to my growing sense of alienation. *Would any girl ever want a boyfriend who couldn't hold her hand or dance with her?*

Without even being aware of it, I allowed those dark thoughts and negative feelings to burden my spirit with growing frequency. Often they came creeping into my mind late at night when I couldn't sleep, or when I was tired after a long day at school. You know the feeling; you are so weary and out of sorts that the whole world seems to be weighing on your shoulders. We all experience down times, especially when lack of sleep, illness, and other challenges make us vulnerable.

No one is happy and perky one hundred percent of the time. Your more somber moods are natural. They serve a purpose too. According to recent psychological studies, a darker mood can make you look at your work more critically and analytically. That outlook is helpful when you are involved in tasks like balancing your checkbook, figuring out your taxes, or editing a paper. As long as you are aware and in control of your emotions, negative thoughts can produce positive consequences. Only when you let your emotions control your actions do you risk spiraling down into depression and self-destructive behaviors.

The key is to refuse to be overwhelmed or swept away by negative emotions or feelings of depression. Fortunately, you have that power to adjust your attitude. When you detect negative thoughts running through your mind, you can choose to hit the "off" switch. Acknowledge them and understand their source, but stay focused on the solutions instead of on the problems. I remember from Bible class a picture of the "whole armor of God" with the breastplate of righteousness, the belt of truth, the shield of faith, the sword of the Spirit, and the helmet of salvation. I'd learned that those were all the weapons that a Christian boy would ever need. I see the word of God as a sword to fight negative thoughts. The sword is the Bible. You also hold up the shield of faith to defend yourself.

SPIRAL OF DESPAIR

At that critical age of adolescence when self-esteem and self-image are so important, I let my worries and fears overtake me. Everything that was wrong with me overpowered all that was right.

I drew the short straw. How will I ever lead a normal life with a job, a wife, and kids? I will always be a burden to those around me.

I was never crippled until I lost hope. Believe me, the loss of hope is far worse than the loss of limbs. If you have ever experienced grief or depression, you know just how bad despair can be. More than ever I felt angry, hurt, and confused.

I prayed, asking God why He couldn't give me what He'd given everyone else. *Did I do something wrong? Is that why you don't answer my prayers for arms and legs? Why won't you help me? Why do you make me suffer?*

Neither God nor my doctors could explain to me why I'd been born without arms or legs. The lack of an explanation, even a scientific one, only made me feel worse. I kept thinking that if there was some reason, spiritual, medical, or otherwise, it might be easier to handle. The pain might not be so great.

Many times I felt so low that I refused to go to school. Self-pity hadn't been a problem before. I had been constantly striving to overcome my disability, to do normal activities, to play as other kids played. Most of the time I impressed my parents, my teachers, and my classmates with my determination and self-sufficiency. Yet I harbored hurt inside.

I'd been raised as a spiritual kid. I'd always gone to church and believed in prayer and God's healing power. I was so into Jesus that when we had dinner, I'd smile, thinking of Him with us there at the table, sitting in our empty chair while we ate. I prayed for arms and legs. For a while I expected to wake up some morning with arms and legs. I'd settle for just getting one arm or leg at a time. When they did not appear, I grew angry with God.

I thought I'd figured out God's purpose in creating me, which was to be His partner in a miracle so the world would recognize that He was real. I would pray: "God, if you gave me arms and legs, I would go around the world and share the miracle. I would go on national television and tell everyone what had happened, and the world would see the power of God." I was telling Him that I got it and was willing to follow through on my end. I remember praying, *God, I know You made me this way so You could give me arms and legs and the miracle would prove to people Your power and love.*

As a child, I learned that God speaks to us in many ways. I felt he might answer me by placing a feeling in my heart. But there was only silence. I felt nothing.

My parents would tell me, "Only God knows why you were born this way." Then I'd ask God, and He wouldn't tell me. These unfulfilled appeals and unanswered questions hurt me deeply because I had felt so close to God before.

I had other challenges to face. We were moving a thousand miles north, up the coast to Queensland, away from my huge family.

My protective cocoon of aunts and uncles and twenty-six cousins was being stripped away. The stress of moving was wearing on my parents too. Despite their assurances and their love and support, I couldn't shake the feeling that I was a tremendous burden to them.

It was as though I'd put on dark blinders that prevented me from seeing any light in my life. I couldn't see how I could ever be of use to anyone. I felt I was just a mistake, a freak of nature, God's forgotten child. My dad and mum did their best to tell me otherwise. They read to me from the Bible. They took me to church. My Sunday school teachers taught that God loves us all. But I couldn't move beyond my pain and anger.

There were brighter moments. In Sunday school I felt joy when I joined my classmates singing, " 'Jesus loves the little children, all the children of the world, red and yellow black and white, they are precious in His sight, and Jesus loves the little children of the world.' " Surrounded by people who supported and loved me, I took that hymn to heart. It comforted me.

I wanted to believe that He cared for me deeply, but then when I was tired or not feeling well, the dark thoughts would creep in. I'd sit in my wheelchair on the playground wondering: *If God really loves me like all the other children, then why didn't He give me arms and legs? Why did He make me so different from His other children?*

Those thoughts began to intrude even during the day and in normally happy circumstances. I'd been struggling with feelings of despair and the sense that my life was always going to be difficult. God didn't seem to answer my prayers.

One day I sat on the high kitchen countertop, watching my loving mum cook dinner, which I usually found reassuring and relaxing. But suddenly these negative thoughts overcame me. It struck me that I didn't want to stick around and be a burden to her. I had the urge to throw myself off the counter. I looked down.

I tried to work out what angle I should use to make sure I snapped my neck and killed myself.

But I talked myself out of doing it, mostly because if I failed to kill myself, I'd have to explain why I was in such despair. The fact that I came so close to hurting myself that way frightened me. I should have told my mother what I'd been thinking, but I was embarrassed. I didn't want to scare her.

I was young, and even though I was surrounded by people who loved me, I didn't reach out and tell them the depth of my feelings. I had resources but didn't use them, and that was a mistake.

If you feel overcome by dark moods, you don't have to handle it yourself. Those who love you won't feel burdened. They *want* to help you. If you feel you can't confide in them, reach out to professional counselors at school, at work, in your community. You are not alone. I was not alone. I see that now, and I don't want you to ever come as close as I did to making a fatal mistake.

But at that time I was becoming swept up in hopelessness. I decided that to end my pain, I had to end my life.

A CLOSE CALL

One afternoon after school I asked my mother if she could put me in the bath to soak for a while. I asked her to shut the door when she left the bathroom. Then I put my ears under water. In the silence, very heavy thoughts ran through my mind. I had planned in advance what I wanted to do.

If God will not take away my pain and if there is no purpose for me in this life . . . if I'm here only to experience rejection and loneliness . . . I'm a burden to everyone and I have no future . . . I should just end it now.

As I mentioned when I described learning to swim, I'd float on my back by filling my lungs with air. Now I tried to gauge how much air to keep in my lungs before I flipped over. *Do I hold my breath before I turn over? Do I take a full deep breath, or do I just do half? Should I just empty my lungs and flip over?*

I finally just turned and plunged my face under water. Instinctively, I held my breath. Because my lungs were strong, I stayed afloat for what seemed like a long time.

When my air gave out, I flipped back over.

I can't do this.

But the dark thoughts persisted: *I want to get out of here. I just want to disappear.*

I blew most of the air out of my lungs and flipped over again. I knew I could hold my breath for at least ten seconds, so I counted down ... *10 ... 9 ... 8 ... 7 ... 6 ... 5 ... 4 ... 3 ...*

As I counted, an image flashed in my mind of my dad and mum standing at my grave crying. I saw my seven-year-old brother, Aaron, crying too. They were all weeping, saying it was their fault, that they should have done more for me.

I couldn't stand the thought of leaving them feeling responsible for my death for the rest of their lives.

I'm being selfish.

I flipped back over and drew a deep breath. I couldn't do it. I couldn't leave my family with such a burden of loss and guilt.

But my anguish was unbearable. That night in our shared bedroom, I told Aaron, "I'm planning to commit suicide when I'm twenty-one."

I thought I could stick it out through high school and university maybe, but I couldn't see myself beyond that. I didn't feel like I could ever get a job or get married like other men. What woman would want to marry me? So the age of twenty-one seemed like the end of the road for me. At my age, of course, it also seemed like a long time away.

"I'm telling Dad you said that," my little brother replied.

I told him not to tell anyone and closed my eyes to sleep. The next thing I knew, I felt the weight of my father as he sat down on my trundle bed.

"What is this about you wanting to kill yourself?" he asked.

In a warm and reassuring tone, he talked to me about all the good things awaiting me. As he spoke, he combed my hair with his fingers. I always loved it when he did that.

"We will always be here for you," he reassured me. "Everything is going to be okay. I promise we will always be here for you. You are going to be fine, son."

A loving touch and caring gaze is sometimes all it takes to put a child's troubled heart and confused mind at ease. My father's reassurance that things would be okay was enough in that moment. He convinced me with his comforting tone and touch that he believed we would find a path for me. Every son wants to trust his father, and that night he gave me something to hold on to. To a child, there is no assurance like a father's. My dad was generous with such things and good at expressing his love and support for all of us. I still didn't understand how everything would work out for me, but because my daddy told me they would, I believed they would.

I slept soundly after our talk. I still had occasional bad days and nights. I trusted my parents and held on to hope for a long time before I actually formed any vision of how my life might unfold. There were moments and even longer periods of doubt and fear, but fortunately this was the lowest point for me. Even now I have my down times like anyone else, but I never again considered suicide. When I look back on that moment and reflect on my life since, I can only thank God for rescuing me from my despair.

HOLDING ON TO HOPE

Through my speaking engagements in twenty-four countries, DVDs, and millions of YouTube.com views, I've been blessed to reach so many with a message of hope. Think about just how much joy I would have missed experiencing if I had taken my life at the age of ten. I would have missed the extraordinary opportunity of sharing my story and what I'd learned with more than 120,000 people in India, another 18,000 in a bullring in Colombia, and 9,000 during a thunderstorm in Ukraine.

In time I came to understand that even though I didn't take my life that dark day, *God did.*

He took my life and gave it more meaning and more purpose and more joy than a ten-year-old boy could ever have understood.

Don't you make the mistake I nearly made.

If I had remained facedown in six inches of water back in 1993, I might have ended my temporary pain, but at what cost? That despairing child could not possibly have foreseen the joyful man swimming with great sea turtles off the Hawaiian coast, surfing in California, or scuba diving in Colombia. Even more important than those adventures are the many lives I might never have touched.

I'm just one small, tiny example. Pick any true-life hero, whether it's Mother Teresa, Mahatma Gandhi, or the Reverend Martin Luther King and you'll find someone who had to weather adversity—prison, violence, even the threat of death—but held on to the belief that their dreams could prevail.

When negative thoughts and dark moods come to you, remember that you have a choice. If you need help, reach out for it. You are not alone. You can choose to picture better days and to perform actions that will make them real.

Consider what I was up against as a boy and look at my life now. Who knows what great days and wonderful achievements await you? Who knows how many lives we can make better by serving as someone else's miracle? So walk with me, the man with no arms and no legs, into a future filled with hope!

THREE

Full Assurance in the Heart

Faith is defined in the Bible as the substance of things hoped for, the evidence of things not seen. You and I could not live without faith, without putting our trust in something for which we have no proof. Most often we talk about faith in terms of religious beliefs, but there are many other types of faith that are part of each day. As a Christian, I live according to my belief in God. Even though I can't see Him or touch Him, I know in my heart that He exists, and I put my future in His hands. I don't know what tomorrow holds, but because I believe in Him, I know who holds tomorrow.

That is one form of faith. I have faith in many areas of my life. I accept that there are certain elements I can't see, touch, or feel, but I believe in them anyway. I trust that oxygen exists, and I trust that science is correct in saying that we need it to survive. I can't see, touch, or feel oxygen. I just know it is there because *I* am here. If I am alive, then I must be breathing it, so oxygen must exist, right?

Just as we must have oxygen to live, we must trust in certain unseen realities to survive. Why? Because we all face challenges. You have them. I have them. There simply are times in our lives when we can't see a way out, and that is where faith comes in.

I received an e-mail recently from a woman named Katie who had been laid off from her job because of her medical problems, which have included nearly twenty surgeries. She'd been born without a femur bone in one leg, which had to be amputated when she was a toddler. Now in her thirties and married, Katie told me she often struggled with the "Why me?" question.

After watching one of my videos, Katie realized that sometimes we just cannot know "Why me?" We must trust that God's plan for us will be revealed in time. Until then we must walk in faith.

"I thank you with all my heart. I now believe that I, like you, am God's chosen one," she wrote. "One day I hope I'll have the honor of meeting you in person to wrap my arms around, hug, and thank you for helping me open my eyes to see the light."

Katie found strength and hope only after she decided to trust in what she could not see or understand. That's exactly how faith works. You will encounter challenges that initially seem insurmountable. While we wait for a solution, faith may be all we have to hang on to, and sometimes simply trusting that there will be an answer will get you through those darkest moments.

That is why I talk about FAITH as an acronym: Full Assurance In The Heart. I may not be able to produce evidence for all that I believe in, but I feel fully assured in my heart that I am much closer to the truth by living with faith than I would be by living in despair. When I talk to thousands of schoolchildren each year, I often explore the notion of trusting in what we can't see. (Sometimes the little ones are a bit frightened of me at first. I don't know why because we're always about the same height. I tell them I'm small for my age.)

I joke with them until they feel comfortable with me. Once they're accustomed to my lack of limbs, I find most kids are fascinated by my little left foot. I'll see them pointing or staring, so I wave it at them and make a joke about "my little chicken drumstick." That always gets a laugh because the description is quite accurate.

My sister, Michelle, who is six years younger than me, was the first to make that observation. With our brother, Aaron, and our parents, we often traveled on long family trips in which we three kids were packed like cordwood in the backseat of the car. Like most dads, ours didn't like to stop once we hit the road. When we grew hungry, we'd drop big hints to my dad and mum.

When we were absolutely famished, we'd go a little crazy and pretend to take bites out of each other. On one trip Michelle announced that she intended to chew on my little left foot "because it looks just like a chicken drumstick." We laughed about it, but I forgot about her description. Then a few years ago, Michelle brought home a puppy. The little pup tried to chew on my foot whenever I sat down. I'd nudge him away, but he kept coming back to gnaw on it.

"See, it still looks like a chicken drumstick even to my puppy!" Michelle said.

I loved it! Ever since then, I've told that story in my speeches to schoolchildren. But once I introduce my left foot, I ask kids if they think I have just one foot. This question always throws them for a loop because they can see only one foot, but it would make sense for me to have two.

Most kids go with what they can see. They usually tell me they think I have just one foot. I then produce for them Junior, my even smaller right foot, which I normally keep tucked in. Sometimes I shock them by sticking out my right foot and wiggling it. They usually shriek and scream. It's funny because kids are so straightforward. They admit that they have to see it to believe it.

I then encourage them, just as I now encourage you, to trust that there are *possibilities* for your life. The key to moving forward, even in hard times, is to let your vision for your life be guided not by what you can see but by what you can imagine. That's called having faith.

TRUST IN FLIGHT

My imagination flows through God's eyes. I trust Him. I have full
assurance in my heart that even without arms and legs, I can build
a wonderful life. In the same way, you should feel that nothing is
out of your reach. Have faith that if you do everything you possibly
can to achieve your dreams, your efforts will be rewarded.

Sometimes our trust is tested before our hard work pays off. I
was reminded of this in 2009 while on a speaking tour of Colombia, in South America. I was booked to speak in nine cities in ten
days. With so many miles to cover in such a limited amount of
time, the tour booker chartered a small airplane to take us from
town to town. There were eight of us on the flights, including our
two pilots, both of whom were named Miguel and neither of whom
spoke much English. During one of the flights, everyone in the passenger cabin was startled to hear the plane's computer call out an
automated warning: "Pull up, pull up!" The alert was in English!

The computer voice tracked our rapid descent with increasing urgency, giving our plane's decreasing altitude. "Six hundred
feet!" "Five hundred feet!" "Four hundred feet!" The reports were
interspersed with continuing commands to the pilots to "Pull up!
Pull up!"

No one freaked out, but the mood in the passenger cabin was
more than a little tense. I asked my caregiver if he thought we
needed to be translating the onboard computer warnings from English to Spanish for Captains Miguel One and Two.

"Do you think they really don't know we're descending?" he
asked.

I didn't know what to think, but since no one else seemed to feel
it was a problem, I followed their lead and tried not to freak out.
Much to my relief, we soon landed safely. Later when one of our
translators mentioned our moment of panic to our pilots, they had
a great laugh.

"We knew what the computer was saying, but we always ignore it when we're landing," Miguel Two said through the translator. "You should have more faith in your pilots, Nick!"

Okay, I'll admit, for a minute there I questioned my trust in the flying Miguels. But most of the time I rest assured that God is looking out for me and my life. I'll give you a clue about the strength of my trust: I have a pair of shoes in my closet! I truly believe it is possible that someday I will be able to wear them and walk in them. It may happen. It may not. But I believe the possibility is there. If you can imagine a better future, you can believe it. And if you believe it, you can achieve it.

Unlimited vision.

When I went through my period of depression as a ten-year-old, I wasn't suffering from anything physically. I had no arms and no legs, but I had all I needed to live the rewarding and fulfilling life I have today—with one exception. Back then I was relying only on what I could see. I was focused on my limitations rather than on my possibilities.

We all have limitations. I'll never be an NBA star, but that's okay because I can inspire people to be the stars of their own lives. You should never live according to what you lack. Instead, live as though you can do anything you dream of doing. Even when you suffer a setback or a tragedy, there is often an unexpected, totally improbable, and absolutely impossible benefit to be realized. It may not happen right away. You may at times wonder what good could possibly come of it. But trust that it all happens for the good—even tragedies can turn into triumphs.

SURF'S UP

I was in Hawaii for a speaking engagement in 2008 when I met the world-class surfer Bethany Hamilton. You may recall that she lost her left arm when she was attacked by a tiger shark in 2003.

She was just thirteen years old when that happened. Prior to the shark attack, Bethany was well known among surfers, but after she survived that tragedy and returned to her sport praising God and thanking Him for his blessings, she became admired internationally for her courageous spirit and her amazing faith. Now, like me, she travels the globe to inspire people and to share her beliefs.

Her goal, she said, is "just to tell about my faith in God and to let everyone know that He loves them and to explain just how much He took care of me that day. I shouldn't be here because I lost seventy percent of my blood that morning."

I'd never heard the whole story of what happened that day until our meeting, and I had not realized how close this awesome young lady came to dying. She told me how she prayed as they rushed her to a hospital forty-five minutes away and how her paramedic whispered encouraging words of faith into her ear: "God will never leave you or forsake you."

Things were looking pretty grim. When they finally arrived at the hospital and hurriedly prepped her for surgery, they found that all of the operating rooms were being used. Bethany was fading fast. But one patient gave up his knee surgery, which was just about to get under way, so his doctor could operate on Bethany. Guess who it was?

Bethany's own dad!

Amazing, isn't it? The surgeon was prepped and ready to operate, so they just switched daughter for dad and went to work. The operation saved her life.

Since she was such a healthy, athletic girl and had such an amazingly positive attitude, Bethany bounced back faster than any of her doctors expected. She was surfing again just three weeks after the attack.

During our visit Bethany told me that her faith in God led her to conclude that losing her arm was part of His plan for her life. Instead of feeling sorry for herself, she just accepted it and moved on. In her first competition against many of the world's best women surfers, she finished third—with only one arm! She says that the loss of her arm is a blessing in many ways because now whenever she does well in a competition, it inspires other people that their lives have no limits!

"God has definitely answered my prayer to use me. He speaks to people when they hear my story," she says. "People tell me that they have drawn closer to God, started to believe in God, found hope for their lives, or were inspired to overcome a difficult circumstance. I just praise God when I hear that because it's not me doing anything for them—God is the One Who is helping them. I'm so stoked that God would let me be a part of His plan."

You can't help but be stoked by Bethany's incredible spirit. Few would have blamed her if she'd quit surfing altogether after the shark attack. She had to learn how to balance on a surfboard all over again, but that didn't faze her either. She trusted that even though something terrible had happened to her, good could come of it.

RIDING THE WAVES

Remember this amazing girl's faith whenever life jumps up and takes a bite out of your plans and dreams. It will happen. We all get hit by unexpected waves now and then. Chances are your problem won't be a shark, but whatever knocks you down, think of this gritty teenage girl who not only survived an attack from one of nature's most ferocious predators but bounced back more determined than ever to lead an awesome life.

Bethany inspired me so much that I asked her to help me do something I'd always wanted to try. Would she teach me to surf? To my amazement, she promptly offered to take me out on Waikiki Beach.

I was psyched at the prospect of learning to surf in the historic place where Hawaiian kings and queens first rode atop waves. I also was more than a little nervous. As Bethany waxed a longboard for me, she introduced me to surfing stars Tony Moniz and Lance Hookano, who would be joining us in the water.

As I've mentioned, when you find yourself wondering whether you will be able to accomplish your goals in life, trust in people who are willing to lend you a hand and who can serve as your guide. That's exactly what I did in approaching this goal. I could not have asked for better surfing buddies. They started me practicing by balancing on my board in the grass.

They took turns riding with me, giving me instructions and cheering me on. As we were wading into the ocean waves, I was struck by the scary thought that the two of us had only three limbs between us—and they were all Bethany's! I loved the idea of being a surfer dude, and as a strong swimmer, I have no fear of the water, but I wasn't sure I could stay on a board atop the waves even with all the expert help. On one trip I did a 360-degree turn with one of my instructors on board. On another I hopped off my board and onto Bethany's board while surfing!

Eventually I wanted to try it by myself. I can't help it—I'm a ham. Finally everyone agreed I was ready to surf solo. To help me get up on my own once I caught a wave, they created a small platform by duct-taping a few folded towels to the front of my surfboard, which I felt confident would help me bring myself up. Then, once I built up some speed on a wave, I could leverage my shoulders against the towels and inch up into a standing position. Where there is a will and a wave, there is a way!

A surfing competition was being held that day at Waikiki, and a crowd began to gather, watching us. Though it made me nervous, I was getting plenty of advice from the experts.

"Are you really going to try this on the water, dude?"

"Dude, I don't know how you can stay balanced without arms and legs!"

"Can you swim, dude? Can you swim faster than a shark, dude?"

Once we were out on the water, I actually felt better. I am very buoyant, so floating and swimming is not a problem. I also tend to drift, so I never know where I might end up. I had visions of floating back to Australia and washing up in my parents' backyard!

It was a gorgeous day. Bethany was in the water alongside me, encouraging me, but whenever I tried to catch a wave and stand up, I'd fall off my board. Six times I tried. Six times I wiped out.

I couldn't give up. Too many people were watching. Too many cameras were rolling. I was not about to be featured on YouTube as the disabled dude who couldn't hang two. As a kid I'd spent a lot of time skateboarding, so I was getting a good feel for it. Finally on my seventh attempt I caught a big wave and brought myself up. It was such a thrill, I don't mind telling you that I screamed like a school-girl as I stood atop that board coming into the beach.

Everyone watching along the beach cheered and whistled as I surfed in. I was stoked! I know that because everyone told me, "Dude, you are a stoked dude!"

For the next two hours we caught wave after wave, making nearly twenty rides. There were several photographers on the beach because of the competition, so I became the first rookie surfer ever to be featured on the cover of *Surfer* magazine. I toweled off from a great day on the water.

Later in an interview Lance Hookano made an interesting observation. "I've been on this beach my whole life," he said, "and I've never been a part of something like this. Nick is one of the most stoked people I have ever seen. He loves it. He's got salt water running through his veins. It makes me think anything's possible."

Hold that thought: *Anything is possible.* When you feel wiped out and blown away by a huge challenge, trust that anything is possible. You may not see a way out at the moment. You may feel that the whole world is lined up against you. But believe that circumstances can change, solutions can appear, and help can arrive from unexpected places. Then anything is possible!

If a bloke with no arms and no legs can learn to surf on one of the world's greatest beaches, anything and everything is possible for you!

FAITH TAKES ROOT

One of the most familiar stories from the Bible is the Parable of the Sower. A farmer sows seeds all over the place. Some fall on the road, where birds eat them. Some fall on rock, so they never take root. Others fall into thorny weeds that choke off their growth. Only the seeds thrown on good soil are able to grow and produce a crop and create many more seeds than were originally sown.

We not only receive seeds in our lifetime, we also hold them in the "good soil" of our hearts. When challenges get us down, we can look to our dreams of a better life. These dreams act as seeds for the realities that will come. Our faith is the rich soil that brings those seeds to life.

Those who loved me always encouraged me. They planted seeds in my heart. They assured me that I had blessings that could benefit others. Some days I believed them. Some days I didn't. But they never gave up on me. They knew that at times they were planting on pavement, or in the weeds. Yet they trusted that their seeds would take root.

My family planted seeds every morning as I went off to school: "Have a good day, Nicholas! Do your best and God will do the rest!"

There were days when I'd think, *Yeah, yeah, God has a mean sense of humor because I know I'll be teased today on the playground.*

Sure enough, as soon as I rolled onto the school grounds in my wheelchair, some jerk would be telling me I had a flat tire or that they wanted to use me as a doorstop in the library. *Very funny.*

On those days of discouragement, the supportive words from my parents fell on hard ground. There was nothing to nurture them. I was too bitter at the circumstances I'd been born into.

But in the months and years following my bad trip to the bathtub, more and more of their encouragement fell on fertile ground. Part of it was that I won over my classmates with my determination and outgoing personality. I still had my down days, but I had fewer of them.

The great inspirational author Norman Vincent Peale once said, "Become a *possibilitarian*. No matter how dark your life seems to be, raise your sights and see the possibilities. Always see them, for they are always there."

You may never be a Presbyterian or a Rotarian, but you should always be a card-carrying Possibilitarian. Without trust in the possibilities for your life, where would you be? Where would any of us be? Our hopes for the future give us momentum. They keep us moving forward through the inevitable hard times, the discouragement, and the despair.

My Possibilitarian tendencies showed up early in life. I was six or seven when I wrote and illustrated my first book. The title was *The Unicorn That Had No Wings*. It's no deep mystery where I came up with that concept, but I have to say that my little parable drawn from my own life still offers a nice message about faith. (Don't worry. It's short. I was only six when I wrote it.)

Once there was a mother unicorn who was having a baby. When the unicorn grew, it didn't have any wings.

The mother unicorn said, "What happened to her wings?"

When the unicorn went for a walk, she could see unicorns flying in the sky. Then a little boy came to the unicorn and said: "What happened to your wings?"

The unicorn answered: "I didn't grow any wings, little boy."

Then the little boy said: "I'll try and make you some plastic wings."

It took him an hour to make the plastic wings for the unicorn.

When the boy was finished, he asked the unicorn if he could go on the unicorn's back, and the unicorn said to the boy: "Yes you can."

So they went for a run, then the unicorn started to fly, and the unicorn shouted: "It worked. It worked."

When the unicorn stopped flying, the boy got off the unicorn's back. Then the unicorn went back in the sky. The little boy said to the unicorn. "Congratulations, unicorn!"

The little boy went back home. He told his mum and his two sisters and his brother what had happened to the unicorn.

The unicorn lived happily ever after.

The End

We all wish to live happily ever after. Even if you believe you can handle the hard times and savor the good times, disappointments will occur. But the happy ending should always be your goal. Why not shoot for it?

PATIENCE REWARDED

My team at Life Without Limbs helped me plan a World Outreach Tour in 2008 with the goal of visiting fourteen countries. In the early planning, we set a budget and held a fundraising campaign to cover our expenses for the trip. We didn't have professional fund-raisers on staff then, and we fell far short of our goal. We raised only about one third of what we felt we needed. I forged ahead and started the tour with visits to Colombia, Ukraine, Serbia, and Romania. When I returned home, my advisers were concerned that we didn't have the funds to continue with the rest of the tour.

My uncle Batta is a successful businessman in California, and he serves on my board. He made an executive decision to cancel two major stops on the rest of my planned tour. Money was not the only reason.

"We are getting more and more reports that it might not be safe to travel because of unrest in India, especially Mumbai, and Indonesia," he said. "Since we are short of our budget anyway, I think it would be wise to visit those countries another time."

My uncle is a very wise man, and I didn't argue with him. I told him that I trusted him. Then I went to a speaking engagement in Florida, where there were 450 volunteers just to handle the huge crowd. I was there to inspire them, but my audience charged me up with their enthusiasm. On the way home to California, I was so encouraged by the reception I received in Florida that I felt an overpowering need to continue our world tour as planned.

I prayed and prayed for guidance. I felt that I should go to India and Indonesia despite our insufficient funds and the signs of danger. I believed we could serve others and the rest would take care of itself. Uncle Batta invited me to dinner at his home to discuss my desire to continue based on faith and not on funds.

As we were talking over dinner, I became very emotional about the situation. I just felt so strongly that this was something I needed to do. Uncle Batta understands me and my drive to bring my message to as many people as I can.

"Let's see where the Lord leads us in the next few weeks," he said patiently.

You don't give up when faced with challenges. You don't run away from them either. You assess the situation, look for solutions, and trust that whatever happens, it will come together for the good. Patience is essential. You plant the seeds. You weather the storms.

You wait for the harvest. Mostly when you encounter an obstacle, you don't do anything foolish. You don't bash your head against it. You don't turn around in defeat. You look for the best solution while trusting that every obstacle serves a purpose.

When the money wasn't there to complete our world tour, we didn't rush out and spend money we didn't have. We prayed. We looked for solutions. We believed that if the door remained closed for now, it would one day open to another opportunity.

The important point to remember is that you will always find a way as you keep looking for it. You may have to adjust your goals to the realities. But as long as you keep breathing, you should remember that the possibilities are still there.

That said, I've got to tell you this: We didn't receive a single answer to our prayers for a way to finance the rest of tour. But then an amazing series of events unfolded.

A few days after my dinner with Uncle Batta, a fellow named Bryan Hart, who'd heard me speak in Florida, called and offered our foundation a large sum of money as a gift.

Then our contacts in Indonesia called to say that they'd rented out two stadiums for us in Hong Kong. They promised to make sure our costs were covered if we came.

Two days after that a California charitable organization came up with an even greater sum that covered the remaining costs for the trip!

Within days money was no longer an issue. We still had security concerns about some of the places where we were going, but we put our trust in God.

SAVING GRACE

Remember when I said it all came together for the good? Because of the money shortage, we had changed our schedule for India, but when funding became available, we rescheduled our visit there and actually made it a week earlier.

That change in schedule may well have saved our lives. Just a couple days after we were in Mumbai, three of the locations we visited were hit by terrorists. The Taj Hotel, the airport, and the southern Mumbai train station were among their targets in attacks that killed 180 people and left 300 injured.

Our original schedule would have had us in Mumbai, at those very locations, during those attacks. You might say we were lucky, but I believe God had a plan that we could not see. That is why it is so important to have faith in the future and to keep working toward your goals even when the odds seem stacked against you.

A FOOT UP ON LIFE

I began this chapter talking about my left foot, a very useful little appendage. I've learned to be very thankful for my left foot because innovators are busy inventing nifty gadgets that work just perfectly for it. Joysticks and touch screens are some of the handiest foot devices to come my way. Even without arms and legs, I can now experience life in ways that my parents and I never would have imagined when I was a child. Though the possibilities for my life may have seemed narrow back then, the limits have been fading away thanks to modern technology and the power of believing and achieving.

As difficult as your life can be, as cruel and unrelenting as it may get, you should hang in there. My situation seemed bleak when I first came into this world, but I have managed to carve out a fulfilling life with many rewards. And if you think I'm an exception, consider the accomplishments of one of my personal heroes, the late Christy Brown.

Born in Dublin, Ireland, in 1932, Christy was the tenth of

twenty-two children in his family, though only thirteen of them survived to adulthood. Christy entered the world with all his limbs, but he was terribly crippled, so much so that he could not move and could only barely utter sounds. At the time the doctors did not know what was wrong with him. Years later he would be diagnosed with an especially severe form of cerebral palsy.

Because Christy could not speak clearly, doctors thought for years that he was mentally handicapped too. His mother insisted that he had no problems mentally—he just could not communicate. She and other family members worked and worked with him. Then one day while Christy was trying to get something across to his sister, he grabbed a piece of chalk from her with his left foot. Due to his physical disabilities, it was the only part of his body he could control.

Christy learned to write, draw, and paint with his left foot. His family, like mine, was determined to give him as normal a life as possible, so they hauled him around in an old go-cart and then in a wagon. Like me, he became an avid swimmer. Then his mother met a doctor who helped get him admitted to Johns Hopkins Hospital. This doctor later created a hospital for Christy and other cerebral palsy patients.

He also introduced Christy to literature, and several famous Irish writers inspired Christy to express himself as a poet and author. His first book was a memoir called *My Left Foot*; it was expanded into a best-selling novel, *Down All the Days*, and was made into a movie starring Daniel Day-Lewis (who, by the way, is the son of one of Christy's literary friends, Cecil). Day-Lewis won the best actor Oscar for his portrayal. Christy eventually published six other books and was also an avid painter.

Think of the long dark days Christy Brown and his family spent wondering what quality of life he would ever have. He could move only one small part of his tormented body. He could make only a few sounds. Yet he became a noted writer, poet, and painter and led an amazing life that was depicted in an award-winning movie!

What lies in store for you? Why would you not stick around to see how your story unfolds?

A FULL VIEW

At times in my childhood I had a limited perspective. My vision of my life was so self-centered that I never dreamed there were other people in worse circumstances than mine, people like Christy Brown. Then, around age thirteen, I read a newspaper story about an Australian man who'd been involved in a horrible accident. As I recall, he was paralyzed, unable to move or talk, and confined to a bed for the rest of his life. I couldn't imagine how horrible that would be.

His story helped to open my eyes and expand my vision. I realized that while my lack of limbs posed many challenges, I still had so much to be thankful for, so many possibilities in my life.

There is great power in believing in your destiny. You can move mountains. My awakening to the fullness of possibilities was a gradual process. At age fifteen I heard the story of the blind man in the Gospel of John. He'd been blind since birth, and when the followers of Jesus saw him, they asked their leader, "Who sinned, this man or his parents, that he was born blind?"

It was the same question I had asked myself. *Did my parents do something wrong? Did I do something wrong? Why else would I have been born without arms and legs?*

Jesus replied, "Neither hath this man sinned, nor his parents." Rather, he was born blind "but that the works of God should be made manifest in him."

When the blind man heard that explanation, it changed dramatically his vision of his life and the possibilities for it. You can imagine how this parable resonated with me as a teenager, so aware of being different, of being disabled, of being reliant on others. Suddenly I saw a new possibility. I was not a burden. I was not deficient. I was not being punished. I was custom-made for God's works to be made manifest in me!

When I read that Bible verse at age fifteen, a wave of peace swept over me as I'd never known before. I'd been questioning why I was born without limbs, but now I realized that the answer was unknowable to anyone but God. I simply had to accept that and believe in the possibilities that He would present for me.

No one knows why I was born with my disability, just as no one knew why that blind man was born with his. Jesus said it had been done so that the works of God might be revealed.

Those words gave me a sense of joy and a feeling of great strength. For the first time I realized that the fact that I couldn't understand why I have no limbs didn't mean that my Creator had abandoned me. The blind man was healed to serve His purpose. I wasn't healed, but my purpose would be revealed in time.

You must understand that sometimes in life you won't get the answers you seek right away. You have to walk by faith. I had to learn to trust in the possibilities for my life. If I can have that trust, you can too.

Think about it: I had no way of knowing, as a boy, that my lack of limbs would help me offer my message of hope in so many nations and to so many diverse people. The hard times and the discouragements are not fun. You don't have to pretend to enjoy them. But believe in the possibilities for better days ahead, for a fulfilling and purposeful life.

A ROLE MODEL

The first time I really witnessed the power of believing in one's destiny was during a high school assembly, when I heard my first motivational speaker. He was an American named Reggie Dabbs, and he had a tough job that day. There were fourteen hundred kids in our school assembly. The air was hot and sticky. The cranky sound system crackled and popped and sometimes just quit.

The natives were restless, but he totally captivated us with his story, telling us that he'd been born to an unmarried teenage Louisiana prostitute who had considered abortion to solve her "little problem." Fortunately for Reggie, she decided to give birth to him. She had no family and no place to live once she became pregnant so she moved into a chicken coop.

Huddled there one night, scared and alone, she remembered that a former teacher, a very sympathetic woman, had told her to call if she ever needed help. That teacher's name was Mrs. Dabbs. She drove from her home in Tennessee to Louisiana, picked up the pregnant teen, and took her home to her own family, a husband and six grown children. Mrs. Dabbs and her husband adopted Reggie and gave him their last name.

The couple instilled in him strong moral values, Reggie said. One of the primary lessons they taught him was that no matter what his situation or circumstances, he always had the choice of responding in either a negative way or a positive way.

Reggie told us that he'd almost always made the right decisions because he had faith in the possibilities for his life. He didn't want to do bad because he believed there was so much good awaiting him. He especially emphasized something that really hit home with me: "You can never change your past, but you can change your future!"

I took his words to heart. He touched all of us. Reggie also helped plant a seed in my mind about having a career as a public speaker. I liked the fact that this humble guy had a positive impact on such a big, fidgety group of people in just a few minutes. And it was also pretty cool that he jetted about the planet just to talk to people—he got paid to give people hope!

As I left school that day, I thought, *Maybe I'll have a good story like Reggie's to share someday.* I encourage you to accept that you may not be able to see a path right now, but that doesn't mean it's not there. Have faith, your story is still waiting to unfold, and I know it will be incredible!

FOUR

Love the Perfectly Imperfect You

One day during a tour of East Asia, I spoke to more than three hundred top business executives and entrepreneurs in Singapore. After I finished my presentation and as the hall was clearing, a dignified gentleman came rushing toward me. He looked as successful and self-assured as the rest of the distinguished audience, so his first words on reaching me were surprising.

"Nick, help me," he pleaded.

As I came to learn, this accomplished man owned three banks, but he had humbly come to me for help because material wealth offered no protection from the anguish he was going through.

"I have a wonderful daughter who is fourteen, and for some horrible reason every time she looks in the mirror she says she feels ugly," he said. "It's breaking my heart that she can't see that she is truly beautiful. How can I make her see what I see?"

It's easy to understand the man's distress, since the most difficult thing for parents to endure is their children suffering. He was trying to help her get through this self-hatred, which was so important, because if we can't accept ourselves when we are young and healthy, how will we feel when we age and experience the medical problems that come with advancing years? And if we hate ourselves for some random reason, it's quite easy to wind up replacing it with hundreds of other arbitrary and equally invalid ones. Youthful insecurities can send you plunging in a downward spiral if you allow yourself to focus on your flaws instead of your strengths.

The Bible tells us that we are "fearfully and wonderfully made." Why, then, is it so difficult for us to love ourselves just as we are? Why do we so often become burdened with feelings that we are not beautiful enough, not tall enough, not thin enough, not good enough? I'm sure this Singapore father lavished his daughter with love and praise, trying to build her confidence and esteem. Our parents and loved ones can wear themselves out trying to build us up, yet it only takes one mean remark from a classmate or nasty comment from a boss or co-worker to undo their efforts.

We become vulnerable and fall into the victim's mentality when we base how we feel about ourselves on other people's opinions or compare ourselves with others. When you are unwilling to accept yourself, you are less willing to accept others, and that can lead to loneliness and isolation. One day I was speaking to a group of teens about how the desire to be popular often leads people to shun the less attractive or athletic kids in school. To make my point, I asked a straightforward question: "How many of you would like to be *my* friend?"

To my relief, most of the people in the room raised their hands.

But then I asked a question that threw them off: "So it doesn't matter how I look, right?"

I let it sink in for a few minutes. We'd just been talking about how kids spend so much time trying to fit in by wearing just the right clothes, having a cool haircut, and being not too heavy, not too thin, not too tan or too white.

"How can you want to be friends with a guy with no arms and no legs—the most different guy you'll probably ever meet—but then reject classmates because they don't have the right jeans, or a clear complexion, or a body suited for the fashion runway?"

When you judge yourself harshly or put intense pressure on yourself, you become judgmental of others. Loving and accepting yourself as God loves you opens the door to a much greater sense of peace and fulfillment.

The pressures that teens and young adults feel seem to be universal. I've been invited to address young people in both China and South Korea because of concerns about high levels of depression and suicide in those rapidly developing, hard-working nations.

I arrived in South Korea just as the 2010 Winter Olympic Games were getting under way in Vancouver. It was fun to see the national pride and enthusiasm of people everywhere in Seoul when Kim Yu-Na, South Korea's "queen" of figure skating, captured her country's first Olympic figure-skating gold medal. Interest was so high in her quest that during her final performance trade on the country's stock market fell to half its normal level.

I had been featured in a documentary that was seen widely throughout South Korea's large Christian population, which led to several invitations to speak. The explosion of faith there is amazing. My hosts at the Onnuri Church told me that South Korean Christians are passionate for missionary work. They predicted that within a decade or two South Korean missionaries would outnumber North American missionaries, which is remarkable given that South Korea is so much smaller.

As we drove into Seoul, I was struck by the number of churches. The capital city is said to have the three largest Christian churches in the world. Although just one hundred years ago Christians in South Korea were few, nearly a third of its 48 million people now call themselves Christians. One of the churches I spoke at, the Yoido Full Gospel Church, has more than 800,000 members who attend services at twenty-one churches.

Friends of mine visit South Korea just to tour the churches. The prayer meetings are incredible with out-loud praying and the ringing of bells to signal each new program. Yet even with this strong spiritual growth, the people have high levels of stress because of the strain of long hours at work. The pressure in the schools is also intense because of fierce competition to be the best. Many young people are stressed by the feeling that first place is the only worthy place. If they don't get the top position, they feel they've lost. I encourage them to know that failing an exam doesn't make them failures. We are all of value in God's eyes, and we should love ourselves as He loves us.

The kind of self-love and self-acceptance I'm advocating is not about loving yourself in a self-absorbed, conceited way. This form of self-love is self-*less*. You give more than you take. You offer without being asked. You share when you don't have much. You find happiness by making others smile. You love yourself because you are not all about yourself. You are happy with who you are because you make others happy to be around you.

But what if you just can't love yourself because no one else loves you? I'm afraid that is simply not possible. You see, you and I are God's children. Each of us can count on His unconditional love, His mercy, and His forgiveness. We should love ourselves, be understanding of our imperfections, and forgiving of our mistakes because God does all of that for us.

During a tour of South America I spoke at a drug rehabilitation center in Colombia. The addicts and former addicts in my audience had so little regard for their value as human beings that they'd nearly destroyed themselves with drugs. I told them that God loved them no matter how long they'd been addicted. Their faces lit up when I assured them, through an interpreter, that God loved them unconditionally. If God is willing to forgive our sins and love us like that, why can't we forgive and accept ourselves? Like the daughter of the Singapore banker, these Colombian drug users lost their way because, for whatever reasons, they devalued their lives. They felt they were unworthy of the best that life had to offer. I told them that we are all worthy of God's love. If He forgives us and loves us, we should forgive and love ourselves and then strive for the best life possible.

When Jesus was asked to name the most important commandments, he said the first was to love God with all your heart, soul, mind, and strength, and the second was to love your neighbor as yourself. Loving yourself is not about being selfish, self-satisfied, or self-centered; it's about accepting your life as a gift to be nurtured and shared as a blessing to others.

Instead of dwelling on your imperfections, your failings, or your mistakes, focus on your blessings and the contribution you can make, whether it's a talent, knowledge, wisdom, creativity, hard work, or a nurturing soul. You don't have to live up to anyone else's expectations. You can define your own version of perfection.

SHINE FROM WITHIN

The psychiatrist and author Elisabeth Kübler-Ross said people are like stained-glass windows: "They sparkle and shine when the sun is out, but when darkness sets in their true beauty is revealed only if there is a light from within." To live without limits and especially to survive the darkness of depression, drug addiction, alcoholism, or any major challenge, you must switch on that light within. You must believe in your own beauty and value as someone who can make a difference, someone who matters.

Finding your purpose is the first important step to living a life without limits. Maintaining hope for the future and faith in the possibilities even in difficult times will keep you moving toward that goal. But to be fulfilled, you must know in your heart that you are *worthy* of success and happiness. You must love yourself, just as God loves all who are faithful.

I have a friend who is so comfortable with himself, so at peace and enthused about developing his gifts, that he just seems to radiate good feelings. I love being with him. Everyone loves being with him. Why? Because he shines from within. He loves himself, but not in a "you're so vain" way; he accepts himself as blessed, even when events don't go his way, even though he struggles just like you and me.

I'm sure you know people who give off that same comfortable vibe, just as you probably know the opposite sort of person whose bitterness and self-loathing drive everyone away. If you don't accept yourself, it not only leads to self-destruction, it leads to isolation.

If you don't shine from within, it may be because you rely on others to validate you, to give you confidence, and to make you feel appreciated. But that is a sure road to disappointment because you must accept yourself first. The only important measure of your beauty and value as a person should be the one that comes from within.

I know, easy to say, tough to do. I've struggled with this too. As the child of Christian parents, I'd always been taught that Jesus loved me and that I was created perfectly according to His plan. Of course, all my parents' Bible teachings and all my family's efforts to lift me up came crashing down as soon as one snotty little kid ran up to me and screamed, "You're a freak!"

Life can be cruel. People can be thoughtless or just plain mean. So you must be able to look inside for strength, and when that inner strength fails, you can always look above, to God, the ultimate source of strength and love.

Self-acceptance and self-love are important but often misunderstood concepts these days. You should love yourself as a reflection of God's love and as someone put on this earth to make a unique contribution. Too many teens and adults settle for a more superficial meaning when they buy into the extremes of narcissism and self-indulgence. This is due, in no little part, to the cult of beauty and celebrity promoted on reality shows, movies, podcasts, and videos. When you watch those shows, it is easy to forget that life has a greater purpose than looking good, living in luxury, and hooking up. No wonder more celebrities are in rehab than in church. Too many of them worship the false gods of vanity, pride, and lust.

I can't imagine that any previous generation has been lied to as much as the present ones. We are continually bombarded with messages that we need to have a certain look, a certain car, and a certain lifestyle in order to be fulfilled, loved, appreciated, or considered successful. We've come to a dangerous point in our culture when being in a sex video is considered a path to fame, fortune, and fulfillment.

Don't you think this would be a better world if the paparazzi followed college graduates with advanced degrees, or missionaries bringing medicine and hope to the poor and needy, instead of stalking rehab dropouts with rap sheets and needle scars? But all is not lost. I've seen huge throngs of people, young and old, attend religious ceremonies and festivals of praise, seeking contentment by learning to love their neighbor. I've watched teens and adults spend their vacations building homes in Third World countries and serving the needy in impoverished areas of North America. Not everyone is obsessed with plastic surgery, liposuction, and Louis Vuitton bags.

When you get caught up in material goods and surface beauty, and when you let other people determine your value, you give up too much of yourself and risk letting your blessings go to waste. After watching my DVD, Kristy wrote to me: "You made me realize what's the point of having someone love you if you don't love yourself? I saw you over a year ago and again today. I realized I need to tell you what you have done for me. You have taught me to stand up for myself, love myself for who I am, and just live my life the way I want to live it . . . Oh by the way, now that I have changed the way I feel about myself, my boyfriend has noticed a big difference in me, and he is grateful to you. He was always scared for me, afraid I might do something stupid one day and kill myself. But now I have changed, and my life is so much happier!"

SELF-ACCEPTANCE

My message resonated with Kristy because I've been where she was. When I was seven years old, I went home after one particularly cruel day of rejection and disappointment and spent hours staring into my mirror. Most teens worry about pimples and keeping their hair under control. I had all of the usual challenges on top of the missing limbs.

I really am just a weird-looking bloke, I thought.

Grief overwhelmed me. I allowed myself to wallow in self-pity for a good five minutes. But then a voice from deep inside said, *Okay, like your mum says, you're missing some bits and pieces, but you have some good features too.*

I thought, *Name one. I dare you. Just find one thing, and that will be enough.*

I studied my reflected image a little longer and finally came up with something positive.

I have nice eyes. Girls have told me I have nice eyes. I have that if nothing else! And no one can change that about me. My eyes will never change, so I will always have beautiful eyes.

When you feel your spirits tumbling because you've been hurt or bullied or disparaged, go to the mirror and find one feature you love about yourself. It doesn't have to be a physical characteristic. It can be a talent, a trait, or something else that makes you feel good about yourself. Dwell on that special something for a while. Be grateful for it, and know that your beauty and value come from the unique person you were made to be.

Don't cop out and claim, "There is nothing special about me." We are so hard on ourselves, especially when we compare ourselves unfavorably to others. I see this especially when I talk to teenagers. So many of them struggle with feelings of inadequacy, or the sense that no one will ever love them.

That is why I make it a point to tell them, "I love you just as you are. You are beautiful to me."

Those are simple words from me, a strange-looking stranger. I offer them in most of my speaking engagements for schools and youth groups. My simple words always seem to strike a chord. In fact, the response is usually quite remarkable.

The typical reaction begins with a muffled whimper or a smothered sniffle. I'll look out to see a girl with her head down or a boy with his hands over his face. Then the powerful emotions will sweep through the room like a contagion. Tears will flow down young cheeks. Shoulders shake from stifled sobs. Girls huddle together. Boys leave the room to hide their faces.

The first few times this happened, I was taken aback. *What's going on? Why are they responding so strongly?*

My audience members themselves have answered those questions. After my speeches, young and old, they line up to hug me and share their feelings. Again, the response is overwhelming. Often they line up for hours.

Now, I'm a handsome enough bloke, but people don't stand in lines for hours to hug me because I'm so dashing. What really seems to be drawing them is that I unleash a pair of powerful forces that so many are lacking in their lives: *unconditional love* and *self-acceptance.*

Kristy's is just one of many e-mails and letters I receive and personal conversations I have with people young and old who've thought about taking their lives because they've lost their ability to love themselves. When you are hurt, you build walls to keep from being hurt again, but you can't build an interior wall around your heart. And if you will only love yourself as you are, for all your natural beauty inside and out, others will be drawn to you, and they will see your beauty too.

LOVE YOURSELF ENOUGH TO LAUGH AT YOURSELF

Our friends and loved ones can tell us one hundred times a day that we are beautiful and we are loved and that the hard times will pass, but too often we shrug off the supportive words and hang on to the hurt. I did that for the longest time. My parents would spend weeks trying to undo the damage done by one or two kids who teased me on the playground. But finally when someone my own age reached out, I was transformed. When one girl in my class told me that I was "looking good," I walked on a cloud for a month.

Of course, a short time later, I woke up at thirteen years old with a pimple on my nose. It was not pretty. It was a huge, ripe tomato of a pimple.

"Look at this, it's crazy," I told my mum.

"Don't scratch it," my mum said.

What would I scratch it with? I wondered.

I went to school feeling like the ugliest dude on the planet. Every time I passed a classroom and saw my reflection in the windows, I wanted to run and hide. Other kids stared at it. I kept hoping it would go away, but two days later it was even bigger, the largest and reddest pimple in the universe. I began to think it would one day outweigh the rest of me.

The monstrous deformity would not go away! My humongous zit was still there eight months later. I felt like Rudolph the Red-Nosed Australian. Finally my mum took me to a dermatologist. I told him I wanted the pimple removed even if it took major surgery. He examined it with a huge magnifying glass—as if he couldn't see it—and said, "Hmmmm. It's not a pimple."

Whatever it is, I thought, *let's just get rid of it, shall we?*

"It's a swollen oil gland," he said. "I can cut it off or burn it off, but either way it will leave you with a scar bigger than this little red dot."

Little red dot?

"It's so big I can't see around it," I protested.

"Would you rather be scarred for life?" he asked.

The giant not-a-zit remained on my nose. I prayed and fretted about it for a while, but finally I realized that the bright red bulb on my nose was no more of a distraction than my lack of limbs. *If people aren't willing to talk to me, that is their loss,* I decided.

If I caught someone staring at it, I made a joke. I told them I was growing an extra nose to sell on the black market. When people saw that I could laugh at myself, they laughed with me and empathized. After all, who hasn't had a pimple? Even Brad Pitt has pimples.

Sometimes, through our own doing, we make little problems big by taking them way too seriously. Having a pimple is part of the deal. We are all perfectly imperfect human beings, some of us maybe more than others, but we all have our flaws and our shortcomings. It's important to not take every little wart or wrinkle too seriously because one day you will have something truly serious go wrong, and then what will you do? So stand prepared to laugh at life's little knocks on the heads and bumps on the nose.

Laughter has been shown to reduce stress by releasing endorphin hormones, the body's natural relaxant, boosting your immune system and improving your blood flow while also increasing oxygen to the brain. Not bad, eh? Studies have also shown that laughter makes you more attractive. A double bonus!

BEAUTY IS BLIND

Do you know what is really laughable? Vanity is hilarious, because just as soon as you think you are looking good and sexy and worthy of the cover of *People* magazine, along comes a life lesson to make you realize that beauty really is in the eyes of the beholder, and what is on the outside is not nearly as important as what is on the inside.

Recently I met a young Australian girl who is blind. We were doing a Fun Run to raise money to provide medical equipment for needy kids. This girl was about five years old. Her mum introduced her to me after the event. The mother explained to her that I'd been born with no arms and no legs.

Blind people sometimes ask to touch my body so they can comprehend what someone without limbs is like. I don't mind it, so when this girl asked her mother if she could "see" for herself, I gave permission. Her mum guided her hand over my shoulders and over my little left foot. The girl's reaction was interesting. She was very calm as she felt my empty shoulder sockets and my strange little foot. Then when she put her hands on my face, she screamed!

It was hilarious.

"What? My beautiful face scares you?" I asked, laughing.

"No! It's that hair all over you! Are you a wolf?"

She had never felt a beard before. When she touched my stubble, she freaked out. She told her mother that it was sad I was so hairy! This girl had her own idea of what was attractive, and obviously my beard was not on the list. I wasn't offended. I was glad to be reminded that beauty is definitely in the eyes—and touch—of the beholder.

CELEBRATE YOUR YOU-NIQUENESS

We humans are a silly bunch. We spend half our time trying to fit in with the crowd and the other half trying to stand out from it. Why is that? I'm guilty of it, and I'm sure you are too, because it seems to be universal, part of our human nature. Why can't we be comfortable with ourselves, knowing that we are God's creations, made to reflect His glory?

As a schoolboy, I was desperate to fit in, just as most teens are. Have you ever noticed that even the teens who want to be "different" usually hang out with kids who dress, talk, and act just like them? What's with that, mate? How can you be an *outsider* if everyone you hang with wears the same black clothing, black nail polish, black lipstick, and black eyeliner? Doesn't that make you an *insider* instead?

Tattoos and piercings used to be a rebellious statement of rugged individualism. Now soccer moms in the grocery have tattoos and piercings. There has to be a better way to celebrate your individuality than following the same fads and trends as every mum at the mall, doesn't there?

I've adopted an attitude that might work for you. I've decided that my beauty lies in my differences, in the fact that I'm not like everybody else. I'm uniquely me. Nobody will ever call me "average" or "just another guy." I may not stand tall in a crowd, but I definitely stand out.

That attitude has served me well because I often draw strange reactions from children as well as adults when they see me for the first time. Kids tend to reckon I'm from another planet or I'm some sort of monster. Teens tend to have lurid imaginations so they assume I was maimed by an ax murderer or something equally gruesome. Adults leap to strange conclusions too. Often they suspect that I'm a mannequin or a Muppet.

Once when I was visiting relatives in Canada, they took me trick-or-treating for the very first time. They found a big scary old man mask that covered my entire body, and then they carried me door to door. At first we didn't get much reaction from people, until we figured out that they didn't think I was real. We finally realized this when a woman dropped some of my favorite lollies in my bag, and I said, "Thank you! Trick or treat!"

The woman shrieked and jumped backward. "There's a child in there?" she screamed. "I thought you were carrying a doll!"

Well, I am pretty cute, I thought.

When I'm feeling frisky, I've been known to take full advantage of my uniqueness. I love to cruise around shopping malls with my cousins and friends. One day a few years ago we were in a mall in

Australia when we spotted a window display for Bonds underwear, which is the Down Under version of Haines or Jockey, a briefs brand that has been around for a long, long time.

The male mannequin was wearing a pair of Bonds "tighty whitey" underwear. He had a body just like mine: all head and torso, no limbs—and a nice six-pack of abs. I happened to be wearing my own Bond brand drawers, so my cousins and I decided that I too could serve as a window model. We went into the store. My cousins hoisted me into the window display case. I then took up a position next to the mannequin.

For the next five minutes, I baited mall rats. Whenever window shoppers stopped or glanced at me, I twitched, smiled, winked, or bowed—to their utter shock and horror! Of course, this bit of punking provoked uproarious laughter from my co-conspirators watching from outside the store. Afterward they made the case that if my public speaking career ever faltered, I could always find work as a department store dummy.

LIGHT IT UP

I've learned to laugh about my disabilities and the strange responses they provoke, but there is an even better method for overcoming doubts about your self-worth or your inability to love yourself as you are. Instead of dwelling on that pain within, reach out to ease someone else's pain. Put your focus on someone else in need.

Volunteer at a soup kitchen. Raise money for orphans. Organize a benefit to help earthquake victims. Find sponsors who'll donate money if you take part in a charity walk, or bike ride, or dance marathon. Rise up and reach out.

When I do that, I discover what is perhaps the best solution for anyone who has failed to turn on the light of love within.

If you can't resolve your own issues, be the solution for someone else. After all, it's better to give than to receive, right? If you don't love yourself, then give yourself away. If you do that, you'll be amazed at how valuable you feel.

How do I know that? C'mon, mate, look at me. Look at my life. Do I seem like a happy and fulfilled person to you?

A nose job won't bring you a life of joy. A Ferrari won't make you admired by millions. You already have what it takes to be loved and valued; it's just a matter of releasing and maximizing all that lies within you. You won't always be perfect, and that's perfectly fine. The idea isn't to attain perfection in your lifetime; it's to seek it.

You want to keep striving, keep growing, keep giving all you have to give so that, in the end, you can look back and say, *I gave it my best shot.*

Take a look in the mirror right now and say, "This is who I am, and I accept the challenge of becoming the best I can be." You are beautiful because God created you for His purpose. Your challenge is to find that purpose, fuel it with hope, drive it on faith, and put your *you-niqueness* to the highest possible use.

Loving and accepting yourself is the only surefire cure for self-pity and victimhood. Drugs, alcohol, and promiscuity offer only temporary relief, and eventually they bring only more pain. When I came to see myself as a child of God and a part of His plan, my life was forever changed. You may not be a believer in Christ, but you can believe in your value and purpose on this planet.

BE A FRIEND AND BE HAPPY

My best advice for finding inner happiness is to reach outside yourself, to use your talents and brains and personality to make life better for someone else. I've been on the receiving end of that, and I'm not exaggerating when I tell you that it changed my life.

I was sixteen and a student at Runcorn State High School in Queensland. I usually had to wait an hour or so after school for my ride home. Most days I'd hang out talking to other kids or to a great guy named Mr. Arnold. He wasn't the principal or even a teacher. He was the school janitor. But Mr. Arnold was one of those people who glowed from within. He was so at peace with himself, so comfortable in his coveralls, that everyone respected him and enjoyed being around him.

Mr. Arnold could talk about any subject. He was spiritual and wise. On some days he led a Christian youth discussion at lunchtime. He invited me to join, even though I told him I wasn't big into religion. But I liked him, and so I began attending their sessions.

Mr. Arnold encouraged kids to talk about their lives at these meetings, but I always turned down his invitations. "Come on, Nick, we'd like to hear your story," he'd say. "We want to know more about you and what you're thinking."

For three months I refused. "I don't have a story to tell," I'd say.

Finally Mr. Arnold wore me down. The other kids were very open about their feelings and their experiences, so I finally consented to talk about my own at the next meeting. I was so nervous, I prepared note cards with bullet points. (Nerdy, I know.)

I wasn't expecting to impress anyone. I just wanted to get through it and get out of there, or so I told myself. A part of me also wanted to show the other kids that I had the same feelings, hurts, and fears that they'd expressed.

For ten minutes that day I talked about what it was like to grow up without arms and legs. I told sad stories and funny stories too. I didn't want to seem like a victim, so I talked about my victories. Since this was a Christian group, I did say that there had been times when I felt God had forgotten me, or that I'd been one of His rare mistakes. Then I explained how I'd gradually come to understand that maybe there was a plan for me that I just hadn't figured out yet.

"I'm slowly learning to have more faith that I wasn't a mistake," I said, trying to get a laugh.

In truth, I was so relieved to get through my talk that I felt like crying. To my amazement, most of the kids in the room were crying instead.

"Was I that bad?" I asked Mr. Arnold.

"No, Nick," he said. "You were that good."

At first I thought he was just being nice and the kids in the group were pretending to be moved by my speech. They were Christians, after all. They were supposed to be nice.

But then one of the guys in the group invited me to speak to his church youth group. Then another invitation came from another kid for his Sunday school class. Over the next two years, I received dozens of invitations to share my story to church groups, youth organizations, and service clubs.

I had avoided Christian groups in high school because I didn't want to be labeled as the do-gooder preacher's kid who was all about religion. I acted tough and sometimes cursed so I could be accepted as a regular guy. The truth was that I had not yet accepted myself.

Obviously, God has a sense of humor. He wrangled me into speaking to just the group I had avoided, and it was there that He revealed my purpose in life. He showed me that even if I was not perfect, I had riches to share, blessings to lighten the burdens of others.

The same holds true for you. We share our imperfection. We need to share the beautiful gifts we've been given. Look inside. There is a light inside you just waiting to shine.

FIVE

Attitude Is Altitude

When I created a company to handle my corporate speaking engagements, I named it Attitude Is Altitude because without a positive attitude I never would have been able to rise above my disabilities and reach so many people.

You may be tempted to scoff at the concept of "attitude adjustment" because it has become such a staple of motivational posters and coaching materials. But there is real power in controlling your attitude, adjusting it to counter moods and stop behaviors that may threaten your ability to live without limits. The psychologist and philosopher William James, who taught at Harvard University, said that one of the greatest discoveries of his generation was the realization that *by changing our attitudes, we can change our lives.*

Whether you are aware of it or not, you view the world through your own unique perspectives or attitudes based on your beliefs of what is good or bad, wrong or right, fair or unfair. Your decisions and actions are based on those attitudes, so if what you've been doing isn't working, you have the power to adjust your attitude and change your life.

Think of your attitude as the remote control for your television set. If the program you are watching doesn't do anything for you, then you simply grab the remote and change it. You can adjust your attitude in much the same way when you aren't getting the results you want, no matter what challenges you encounter.

Linda, a music teacher, wrote and described how her amazing attitude helped her overcome a childhood accident that easily could have ruined her life. She was only halfway through grade school when she was severely injured in a car accident. Linda spent two and a half days in a coma, and when she regained consciousness, she could not walk, talk, or eat.

Although doctors feared she would be mentally impaired and never able to speak or walk normally, her mind, speech, and body gradually recovered. In fact, Linda's only remaining medical problem from the horrible accident is a damaged right eye that has only limited vision.

This woman suffered incredible pain, endured many operations, and still has impaired eyesight. She could easily feel victimized and bitter. You could hardly blame her for taking the attitude that life has treated her unfairly. Instead, this is the attitude she chose:

"Sometimes I am frustrated that my eyes don't work in perfect unity with each other," she wrote to me. "But then I remember where I came from and where I could be, and realize God saved me for a reason—to live as a witness to His work in my life. My eye is a reminder from God that I'm not perfect, but that's okay; I need to depend fully on Him for my strength. God chose to show His power through the weakness of my eye—though I am weak, He is strong."

Linda chose to accept her imperfect vision as part of God's "perfect plan for my life," she wrote. "He changed my attitude toward life—I know that mine may very well end at any moment, so I'm trying to live for Him all the time. Also, I try to always put a positive spin on everything, try to give my all to God and others, and truly care about the people around me."

Instead of focusing on her limited vision in one eye, Linda chooses to be grateful that she is able to think, speak, walk, and live a normal life in most ways. You and I have the ability to choose our attitudes just as she chose hers.

You don't have to be a saint to do that. When you experience a tragedy or a personal crisis, it's perfectly normal and probably healthy to go through stages of fear and anger and sadness, but at some point we all have to say: "I'm still here. Do I want to spend the rest of my life wallowing in misery, or do I want to rise above what has happened to me and pursue my dreams?"

Is it easy to do that? No, it is not. It takes great determination, not to mention a sense of purpose, hope, faith, and the belief that you have talents and skills to share. But Linda is just one example of many, many people who've shown what it's possible to overcome with a positive attitude. The age-old, time-proven, undeniable truth is that you and I may have absolutely no control over what happens to us, but we can control how we respond. If we choose the right attitude, we can rise above whatever challenges we face.

You likely will have no control over the next big bad bump in your life. A hurricane hits your house. A drunk driver crashes into your car. Your employer lays you off. Your significant other says, "I need space." We are all blindsided from time to time. Be sad, feel bad, but then pull yourself up and ask, *What's next*? Once you've whimpered awhile, vented, or shed all the tears in your tank, pull yourself together and make an attitude adjustment.

POWERING UP

You can change your attitude and change your life without taking a pill, seeing a shrink, or trekking to a mountaintop to consult a guru. So far in this book I've been encouraging you to find your purpose, to have hope for the future and faith in the possibilities for your life, and to love yourself as you are. Those attributes will give you a strong foundation and reason for optimism, which is the power source for adjusting your attitude, much like the batteries in your television remote control.

Have you ever known a successful, fulfilled, happy person who is also a pessimist? I haven't. That's because optimism is empowering—it gives you control over your emotions. Pessimism weakens your will and allows your moods to control your actions. With an optimistic outlook, you can adjust your attitude to make the best of bad situations. This is sometimes described as "reframing" because while you can't always change your circumstances, you *can* change the way you look at them.

At first, you may have to do this consciously, but once you practice it for a while, it becomes automatic. I am on tour constantly with my caregivers, and in the early days of my speaking career, when a flight was canceled or a connection missed, I had trouble controlling my anger and frustration. Finally I had to face the fact that when you travel as often as we do, there will be problems. Besides, I was getting too old to throw tantrums, and they sort of lose their effectiveness when you can't really stomp your feet.

I had to master the ability to adjust my attitude about travel interruptions. Now when we are forced to sit for hours in airports or need to abruptly change plans, I avoid stress, frustration, and anger by focusing on a positive interpretation of the negative event. I fire up optimistic thoughts such as: *Our flight was delayed because of bad weather. That's good, because we'll have a safer trip if we wait out the storm.*

Or: *They canceled our flight because of mechanical problems. I'd rather wait here on the ground for a good plane than be up in the air in a bad one.*

I'd still rather have a smooth trip than a bumpy one, but the alternative to adjusting my attitude was to dwell on the negative, and that's just not healthy. When you allow circumstances beyond your control to determine your attitude and actions, you risk plunging into a downward spiral of hasty decisions and faulty judgments, to overreacting, giving up too soon, and missing those opportunities that always—always—appear just when you think life will never get better.

Pessimism and negativity will ensure that you never rise above your circumstances. When you feel your blood boiling due to negative thoughts, tune them out and replace them with more positive and encouraging inner dialogue. Here are examples of negative versus positive thinking to help you monitor your own inner voices.

Negative	Positive
I will never get over this.	This too will pass.
I can't take this anymore.	I got this far. Better days are ahead.
This is the worst I've ever had it.	Some days are harder than others.
I'll never find another job.	One door is closed, but another will open.

A HEALING ATTITUDE

My friend Chuck, who is forty years old, learned last year that the cancer he'd fought off twice while in his twenties had reappeared. This time the tumor was so wrapped around vital organs that doctors could not go after it with radiation. The prognosis did not look good—in fact, he was in serious trouble. As a husband and father with a huge circle of family and friends, Chuck had purpose. He also had hope, faith, and self-love working for him. So he adopted the attitude that he was not about to die. In fact, he took on the attitude that while there was sickness inside him, he was not a sick person. He was determined to remain upbeat and positive and focused on moving ahead with his life.

At this point, no one would have described Chuck as a lucky guy, right? Yet the very fact that radiation was not an option turned out to be good luck. You see, Chuck's doctors in St. Louis were taking part in a testing program for an experimental cancer drug that does not use radiation. Instead, this drug targets individual cancer cells and kills them. Since traditional treatments were not suitable for Chuck's tumor, he was eligible for the experimental treatments, but what convinced doctors that he should be in the program was his positive attitude. They knew he would make the most of this opportunity, and he did.

While the experimental cancer drug was being injected in his system through an IV tube, Chuck didn't take it lying down. Instead, he ran on a treadmill. He lifted weights. His attitude was so positive and his energy so high, Chuck had trouble convincing some of the hospital staff that he really belonged on the cancer treatment floor. "You just don't look or act like our normal patient," they said.

A few weeks after receiving his experimental treatments, Chuck met with his doctor. The doctor told him that something strange had happened. "I can't find any sign of the tumor," he said. "It's gone."

Doctors couldn't say whether it was the experimental drug, or Chuck's attitude, or a miracle, or a combination of all three that defeated the tumor. All I can tell you is that Chuck walked out of that hospital free of cancer and strong as a bull. Despite all indications that he was facing death, he chose a positive attitude and focused not on being sick but on his purpose, on hope, on faith, and on the conviction that he could be of benefit to others.

PICK A 'TUDE

Notice that Chuck and Linda both chose attitudes that allowed them to rise above difficult circumstances, but they chose slightly different types of attitudes. Linda chose to be grateful rather than bitter. Chuck chose to take action rather than giving up. There are many attitudes to choose from, but I believe the most powerful are:

1. An attitude of gratitude
2. An attitude of action
3. An attitude of empathy
4. An attitude of forgiveness

1. An Attitude of Gratitude

This is the attitude that Linda unleashed to deal with her injuries from the auto crash. Instead of mourning what she'd lost, she expressed gratitude for what she'd recovered and the life she'd built. I'm a big believer in the power of gratitude. In my speaking I often refer to my little left foot. I do that to put my audiences at ease because they can see my unusual appendage. I joke about it, but I have learned to be very grateful for it. I use it to control my wheelchair joystick, to type on a computer at more than forty words a minute, to play music on my keyboards and digital drum set, and to operate all the applications on my cell phone.

The attitude of gratitude also attracts people who share your enthusiasm and support your dreams. Sometimes these people have the power to inspire you and to change your life in amazing ways. My mum often read to me as a child, and one of my favorite books was *The God I Love*. I was about six years old when she first read it to me. At that time I didn't know of any other person born without arms and legs. I had no role models who looked like me and had the same challenges. This book, which I still think of often, inspired me and helped build the foundation for an attitude of gratitude because it was written by Joni Eareckson Tada.

Joni (pronounced *Johnny*) was an athletic seventeen-year-old swimmer and equestrian from Maryland who was just a few weeks away from her first semester of college when she broke her neck while diving into a lake. She was paralyzed from the neck down in that 1967 accident. In her book she wrote about her initial despair and thoughts of suicide because of her paralysis, but eventually she came to believe that "it wasn't some flip of the coin in the cosmos, some turn in the universe's roulette wheel. It was part of God's plan for me."

I loved that book, and then my mum bought a CD of Joni's songs, which were the first I'd ever heard with lyrics about how "we've all got wheels" and how much fun you could have in a wheelchair and how "nobody's perfect." I played those tapes over and over as a child in Australia, and I still catch myself humming them today. You can imagine how amazing it was when I was invited to meet Joni for the first time.

I was visiting the United States in 2003 to speak at a church in California. After my talk a young woman who worked for Joni introduced herself and invited me to come to the headquarters for her charitable organization, Joni and Friends, in Agoura Hills.

During my visit I was star-struck when she came into the room. She leaned in to give me a hug, and we had this great moment. Joni doesn't have much body strength because of her quadriplegia, so when she leaned in to me she had trouble pulling her body back into her wheelchair. Instinctively, I used my body to give her a gentle push backward into her chair.

"You're very strong!" she said.

I was thrilled to hear that, of course. This amazing woman who had given me strength and faith and hope as a child was telling me that I was strong. Joni shared that, like me, she struggled with her disability at first. She considered driving her wheelchair off a high bridge but worried that she would only injure her brain and make her life even more miserable. Finally, she prayed, *God, if I can't die, show me how to live.*

Shortly after that accident, a friend gave Joni a copy of a Bible verse that says, "In everything give thanks, for this is the will of God and Christ Jesus concerning you." Joni was not deeply religious at the time. She was still angry and frustrated over her paralysis and she wasn't buying that message.

"You can't be serious," Joni said. "I don't feel thankful for this. No way."

Her friend told her that she didn't have to feel thankful for being paralyzed. All she had to do was to take a leap of faith and give thanks for the blessings to come.

It was hard for Joni to buy into that concept. At that point she felt like a victim, and that's what she called herself, "a victim of a terrible diving accident." At first she blamed everyone but herself for her quadriplegia, and she wanted everyone to pay. She sued. She demanded. She even blamed her parents for bringing her into a world in which she could become paralyzed.

Joni felt the world owed her something because she'd lost the use of her arms and legs. She eventually came to realize that victimhood is an easy place to hide. We can all claim to be the victims of one misfortune or another. Some people feel like victims because they were born into poverty. Others claim to be victims because their parents are divorced, or they have poor health, or bad jobs, or they aren't as thin or as tall or as beautiful as they want to be.

When we feel entitled to the good in life, we feel robbed and outraged when something happens to make us uncomfortable. We then look to blame others and demand that they pay for our discomfort, whatever it might be. In a self-centered state of mind, we become professional victims. Yet pity parties are the most tedious, unproductive, and unrewarding events you could ever attend. You can only listen to "Poor, Poor Pitiful Me" so many times before you want to tear your hair out and run for cover.

Like Joni, you should reject the victim role because there is no future in it. She says that suffering brings us to a fork in the road, and we can choose the downward path to despair or we can take the hopeful path up the hill by adopting an attitude of gratitude. You may find it difficult at first to be grateful, but if you just decide not to be a victim and take it day by day, strength will come. If you can't find any aspect of your situation to be grateful for, then focus on good days ahead and express gratitude in advance. This will help build a sense of optimism while getting your mind off the past and looking toward the future.

"I realized that the path away from self-destruction was traced somewhere in the pages of the Bible; and it didn't take long to discover that well-worn truth: 'Take one day at a time in the strength of God and you will become more than a conqueror,' " Joni told me.

Joni discovered that playing the victim only dragged her down further than her paralysis had taken her, but being thankful for the blessings you have and the blessings to come raises you up. That attitude can change your life just as it has changed Joni's and mine. Instead of being angry and resentful over our disabilities, we've built joyful and fulfilling lives.

An attitude of gratitude truly changed her life, and she in turn helped change my life and the lives of so many others who have been helped by her best-selling inspirational books and DVDs. Her Joni and Friends nonprofit organization operates Wheels for the World, a program that has distributed more than sixty thousand free wheelchairs, not to mention thousands of crutches, canes, and walkers, to disabled people in 102 countries.

Joni is a quadriplegic. I have no arms and no legs. Yet we each found a purpose and pursued it. We embraced hope over despair. We put our faith in God and the future. We accepted that we are imperfect human beings with blessings of value. We chose positive attitudes fueled with gratitude, and we put them into action to change our lives and the lives of others.

That's not a poster—it's the truth. By choosing an attitude of gratitude over one of victimhood or bitterness or despair, you too can overcome whatever challenges you face. But if you find gratitude hard to come by, there are other approaches that might work for you.

2. An Attitude of Action

Tabitha has disabilities similar to mine, yet she wrote, "I've always felt blessed and because of this I needed to give back to the universe." Her attitude of action led her and her family to start their own mission to create "goody bags" for children with major ill-nesses and disabilities and for those living in homeless shelters.

Sometimes the best method you'll find for moving your life out of a rut or over an obstacle is to make life better for yourself or for others. Socrates said, "Let him that would move the world, move himself first." When it seems like you can't catch a break, try creating your own. When you've been hit and knocked down by an overwhelming loss or tragedy, allow yourself time to grieve, and then act to create some good out of the bad.

Adopting an attitude of action creates positive momentum. The first steps are the hardest, no doubt about it. Just getting up out of bed may seem impossible at first, but once you are up, you can move forward, and as long as you are moving forward, you are on a path away from the past and toward the future. Go with that. Move ahead step by step. If you've lost someone or something, help someone else or build something else to serve as a memorial and tribute.

One of the most devastating experiences is the loss of a loved one. Losing a family member or a friend triggers grief that can cripple us. Other than perhaps being glad for having loved them and known them and had time with them, there is little to be grateful for in such situations. Nothing prepares us for the grief that can overwhelm and even paralyze us. Still, some take action so that their terrible loss becomes a force for good. A well-known example is Candy Lightner, who channeled her anger and anguish into action after her thirteen-year-old daughter was killed by a drunk driver. She founded Mothers Against Drunk Driving (MADD), which undoubtedly has saved many lives through its activism and education programs.

When tragedies strike us or those we love, the temptation is to go off somewhere and cry, hoping that eventually the heartbreak will ease one day. Yet many people like Tabitha, Joni Eareckson Tada, and Candy Lightner have taken attitudes of action. They believe that even the worst tragedy in their lives can provide opportunities for good deeds. An incredible example of this sort of person is Carson Leslie in Dallas. He was sixteen years old when I met him, but he had been battling cancer for two years already. This young star athlete with a brilliant smile, whose dream had been to play shortstop for the New York Yankees, was just fourteen when he was diagnosed with a brain tumor that had spread to his spine. He underwent surgeries, radiation, and chemotherapy. His cancer went into remission. Then it came back.

Through it all Carson did his best to be a normal kid, living a normal life. He often spoke of his favorite Bible verse, which someone had given him just after he was diagnosed. It's Joshua 1:9: "Have I not commanded you? Be strong and courageous. Do not be terrified; do not be discouraged, for the Lord your God will be with you wherever you go."

Carson was quick to say that this Bible verse was not his "cancer verse" but his "life verse."

"No matter how long I live, I want this verse on my tombstone. And when people visit my grave, I want them to read the verse and think about how it got me through my struggles in life, and I hope others will see that this verse can offer them the same kind of comfort it gives me," Carson wrote in his book, *Carry Me.*

This incredibly brave boy wrote the book with his English teacher to "give a voice to the teenagers and children who have cancer but are unable to express how such an illness affects their personal, social, physical and emotional life." Carson died on January 12, 2010, just as his book was being released. Proceeds go to the Carson Leslie Foundation in support of pediatric cancer research.

How unselfish this young man was. Though he was sick and weary, he spent his final days working on a book to encourage and benefit others. I love too that the final words in his book are these: "None of us know what life has in store . . . but it's easy to have courage when you know the courage comes from God."

I met Carson through Dallas jeweler Bill Noble, a man of deep faith who has often invited me to speak to his church congregation and other groups. Bill's children went to school with Carson, and he brought us together. He called us both "generals in the Kingdom of God."

Aside from teasing me about being "disarming," Bill often stresses the importance of leaving a legacy and making every second count just as Carson did, even at such a young age. Bill used to tell Carson something he'd also told me many times. "God does not define man by his earthly body. As it says in John 6:63: 'The Spirit gives life; the flesh counts for nothing. The words I have spoken to you are spirit and they are life.'"

3. An Attitude of Empathy

If an attitude of action seems beyond your ability, there is yet another option, one that comes from the heart. As I grew more mature and my range of experience expanded, I realized that one of the key factors leading to my thoughts of suicide as a boy was the fact that I was terribly self-centered. I actually believed that no one suffered the emotional pain and physical frustration that I did. My focus was entirely on my own circumstances.

My attitude improved considerably when I grew up a little and realized that many have challenges equal to and greater than my own. When I acknowledged that, I began to reach out to offer encouragement to others with far more empathy. The young daughter of a family friend provided me with a very moving display of empathy on a visit to Australia in 2009. I'd never met the girl, who was only two and a half years old. They'd brought her to a party, and for the longest time she kept her distance, studying me from afar as small children often do. Then, as her parents were preparing to leave, I asked this beautiful child if she wanted to give me a hug.

She smiled and cautiously stepped toward me. Just as she came close enough, she stopped, looked me in the eye, and slowly folded her arms behind her back as if to show solidarity with my lack of limbs. Then she inched forward a little more and placed her head on my shoulder, hugging me with her neck just as she'd seen me hug others. Everyone in the room was struck by this little girl's incredible display of empathy for me. I've been hugged many times, but I can honestly say I'll never forget that hug, because this tiny child obviously has an amazing gift for relating to the feelings of others. Empathy is a great gift. I encourage you to practice and share it at every opportunity because it heals those who give, as well as those who receive. When you are confronted with hard times, tragedies, or challenges, instead of looking inward, look to those around you. Instead of feeling wounded and seeking pity, find someone with greater wounds and help them heal. Understand that your grief or pain is legitimate, but suffering is part of the human condition, and reaching out to someone else is a way of healing yourself while helping others heal too.

My friend Gabe Murfitt understands this as well as anybody I know. We met when I spoke at the Gather4Him fundraising dinner in Richland, Washington, in 2009. Gabe was born with malformed legs and arms that are just three inches long. His thumbs have no bones in them, and he has a hearing impairment. Somehow, he still manages to be extremely active, playing baseball, basketball, and hockey, jumping rope, and banging away on the drums, among other things.

Gabe, who grew up near Seattle, has an indomitable spirit as well as great empathy. Now a college student at Washington State University, he began playing Little League baseball at the age of six. He once climbed Mount Rainier with a group of friends and family members supporting him. Though he had his own challenges in high school, he began reaching out to other students to inspire them by giving his "CLEAR" speeches on courage, leadership, excellence, attitude, and respect. He and his family created a nonprofit organization to help others with disabilities. Gabriel's Foundation of HOPE (http://www.GabesHope.org) provides scholarships and grants as well as encouragement as a result of Gabe's amazing empathy.

Do you see the power in Gabe's attitude of empathy? He took the focus off his challenge and reached out to others. He transformed the challenge of his disabilities into a mission of empathy, enriching his life and those of countless others.

I often am amazed at the way people react to me when I journey into regions of stark poverty and great suffering. I always find men, women, and children who have incredible compassion. Not long ago I was in Cambodia, rushing to get back to my hotel after a long meeting in stifling heat and humidity that made me feel faint. I just wanted to take a shower and sleep for a day or two in an air-conditioned room.

"Nick, before we go, would you mind speaking with this child?" my host said. "He has been waiting outside for you all day."

The boy, smaller than me, was alone, sitting in the dirt. Flies swarmed about him in such numbers that they formed a dark cloud. He had a gaping and deep wound or sore on his head. One of his eyes appeared to be popping out. He smelled of decay and filth. Yet there was such compassion in his eyes, so much love and sympathy—for me—that this child put me completely at ease.

He walked up close to me in my stroller chair and gently put his head against my cheek, trying to soothe me. This boy looked as though he hadn't eaten for days. He appeared to be an orphan who'd suffered greatly. Yet he wanted to express his empathy for what he imagined was my suffering. I was so touched by him that tears flowed.

I asked our hosts if there was anything we could do for this boy, and they promised me that they would see that he was fed, cared for, and given a place to sleep, but after thanking him and returning to our vehicle, I honestly could not stop crying. I could not think straight for the rest of the day. I could not get over the fact that here was this boy whom I'd felt sorry for, but he wasn't focused on his suffering. Instead, he had compassion for me.

I don't know what that child had gone through or how difficult his life was. But I can tell you this: his attitude was amazing because despite all his problems, he still had the ability to reach out and comfort others. What a gift to have such empathy and compassion!

When you feel victimized or self-pitying, I encourage you to adjust your attitude to one of empathy. Reach out to someone else in need. Offer a hand. Volunteer at a shelter. Serve as a guide or a mentor. Use your grief or anger or hurt to help you better understand and ease the pain of someone else.

4. An Attitude of Forgiveness

The fourth attitude you should consider when looking to increase your altitude is an attitude of forgiveness. This may be the best of all, yet it is also the most difficult to learn. Believe me, I know. As I've told you, for a time in my childhood I could not forgive God for what seemed a gross mistake, my lack of limbs. I was angry and in full blame mode. Forgiveness was not on my screen.

Like me, you will have to go through a period of anger and resentment to get to forgiveness. That's natural, but you don't want to hang on to those emotions too long because after a while you only hurt yourself by allowing them to boil within your heart.

Anger was not designed to be an around-the-clock emotion. Like your car, your body breaks down if you keep the engine racing too long. Medical research has shown that harboring anger and resentment for long periods causes physical and psychological stress that weakens your immune system and breaks down your vital organs. And there's another problem with the blame game. As long as my lack of arms and legs was someone else's fault, I didn't have to take responsibility for my own future. Once I made a conscious decision to forgive God and my doctors and move on with my life, I felt better physically and emotionally, and I felt my time had come to take responsibility for the rest of my life.

An attitude of forgiveness set me free. You see, when you hold on to old hurts, you only give power and control to those who hurt you, but when you forgive them, you cut the ties to them. They can no longer yank on your chain. Don't get hung up on thinking that by forgiving them you are doing them a favor; if nothing else, do it for yourself.

I forgave all of those kids who mocked and teased me. I didn't forgive them to absolve them of guilt. I forgave them to unburden myself of anger and resentment. I like myself. I wanted me to be free.

So don't worry about what your forgiveness does for the antagonizers and hurtful people in your past. Just enjoy what forgiving them does for you. Once you've adopted an attitude of forgiveness, you'll lighten your load so that you can chase your dreams without being weighed down by baggage from the past.

The power in forgiveness goes beyond healing yourself. When Nelson Mandela forgave those who imprisoned him for twenty-seven years, the power of his attitude changed an entire nation and had a ripple effect around the world.

This power was unleashed on a smaller scale in the former Soviet Union. When I was in Ukraine, I met a pastor who'd moved his family to Russia to start a church in an area plagued by violence. As word of the pastor's plans spread around town, gangsters issued threats toward him and his five sons, so the pastor prayed.

"God told me that I would pay a steep cost for planting my church there, but that something amazing would result too," he said.

Despite the threats, the pastor established his church. At first few people came to his services. Then, just a week after the pastor opened the doors, one of his sons was murdered on the street. The grieving pastor prayed again, asking for God's guidance. God told him to stay with his church. Three months after his son's death, the pastor himself was stopped on the street by a scary-looking guy who said, "Would you like to meet the person who killed your son?"

"No," said the pastor.

"Are you sure?" the man said. "What if he asked your forgiveness?"

"I've already forgiven him," the pastor said.

"I shot your son," the man said, breaking down. "And I want to join your church."

In the weeks that followed, so many other members of the Russian mob joined the pastor's church that crime all but disappeared in the area. That is the power of forgiveness. When you have a forgiving attitude, you put into motion all sorts of amazing energy. And remember, this attitude allows you also to forgive yourself. As a Christian, I know that God forgives those who seek his favor, but too often we refuse to forgive ourselves for past mistakes, wrong turns, and abandoned dreams.

Self-forgiveness is just as important as forgiving others. I've made mistakes. So have you. We've treated people badly. We've judged them unfairly. We all mess up. The key is to step back, admit you've fallen short, apologize to the injured parties, make a promise to do better, forgive yourself, and move forward.

Now that's an attitude you can live with!

The Bible tells us that we reap what we sow. If you are bitter, angry, self-pitying, and unforgiving, what do you think those attitudes will get you? What joy is there in a life like that? So reject those dark and pessimistic moods, load up on optimism, and charge up an attitude of gratitude, an attitude of action, an attitude of empathy, or an attitude of forgiveness.

I have experienced the power of changing my attitude, and I can tell you that it changed my life, taking me to heights I never imagined. It can do the same for you!

SIX

Armless But Not Harmless

My first and only playground fight was with Chucky, the biggest bully in my grade school. His real name wasn't Chucky, but he had fiery orange hair, freckles, and big ears like the teen-horror-movie Chucky, so I'll call him that to protect the guilty.

Chucky was the first person to put serious fear in my heart. We all deal with fears throughout our lives, both real and imagined. Nelson Mandela said the brave man is not the one who feels fear but the one who conquers it. I certainly felt fear when Chucky tried to knock my block off, but conquering it was another matter.

You couldn't have convinced me of it back then, but your fears and mine are really a gift. Our most basic fears, such as the fear of fire, fear of falling, and the fear of roaring beasts, are hardwired into us as survival tools. So be glad for those fears and own them, but don't let them own you.

Too much fear is not good. Too often our fears of failing or being disappointed or being rejected paralyze us. Rather than face those fears, we surrender to them and limit ourselves.

Don't let fear keep you from chasing your dreams. You should treat fear like you treat your smoke detector. Pay attention to it when it goes off—look around and see if there is real danger or just the alarm ringing. If there is no real threat, put fear out of your mind and go on with your life.

Chucky, my grade-school tormentor, taught me to conquer my fear and move on, but only after the first and last fight of my childhood. I was friends with almost everyone in my school, even the tough kids. Chucky, though, was straight out of the bully factory. He was an insecure kid always on the prowl for someone to pick on. He was bigger than me, but then so was everyone else in the school.

I wasn't exactly a threat to anyone. I was a mere first grader, all of twenty-two pounds, and in a wheelchair. Chucky was a couple years older and a giant compared to me.

"I bet you can't fight," he said one day during morning recess.

My friends were there, so I put on a brave face, but I remember thinking: *I'm in my wheelchair, and he's still twice as tall as me. This is not a promising situation.*

"Bet ya I can" was the best response I could come up with.

It wasn't like I had a lot of experience with fighting. I was from a strong Christian family. I'd been taught that violence was not the answer, but I wasn't a wimp. I'd done a lot of wrestling with my brother and cousins. My little brother still talks about my best wrestling move. Before Aaron grew to be much bigger and taller than me, I could roll him around on the floor and then pin his arm down with my chin.

"You could almost break my arm off with that strong chin of yours," he says. "But then when I got older and bigger, all I had to do was push my hand against your forehead and you couldn't get near me."

That was the problem that I faced with Chucky. I wasn't afraid to fight him, I just didn't know how to get the job done. Every fight I'd seen on television or at the movies involved someone punching or kicking someone else. I lacked the essential hardware for both those moves.

None of this seemed to put off Chucky. "If you can fight, prove it!" he said.

"Okay, meet me on the Oval at lunchtime," I snarled.

"Done," Chucky said. "You'd better be there."

The Oval was an egg-shaped patch of concrete in the middle of our grass and dirt playground. Fighting there was like fighting in the center ring of our school circus. The Oval was our main stage. What happened in the Oval didn't stay in the Oval. If I got whupped in the Oval, I'd never live it down.

All through the morning's spelling, geography, and math classes I fretted about my lunchtime appointment with the school bully. It didn't help that word had spread throughout the school that I was taking on Chucky. Everybody wanted to know my plan of attack. I had no clue.

I kept envisioning Chucky punching my lights out. I prayed that some teacher would find out and stop the fight before we started. No such luck.

The dreaded hour arrived. The lunch bell sounded. My posse gathered around my wheelchair, and we rolled to the Oval in silence. Half the school was there. Some brought their lunches. A few were taking bets.

As you might guess, I was the decided underdog in the early betting.

"You ready to fight?" said Chucky.

I nodded *yes*, but I had no idea how this would go down.

Chucky wasn't so sure either. "Uh, how we gonna do this?" he asked.

"I don't know," I said.

"You gotta get out of your wheelchair," he demanded. "It isn't fair with you in the wheelchair."

Apparently Chucky feared a hit and run. This gave me a negotiating point. Fighting was not my cup of tea, but I was already a good negotiator.

"If I get out of this chair, you have to get on your knees," I said.

Chucky was being razzed about picking on a kid in a wheelchair. He went along with my counterdemand. My stocky foe dropped to his knees, and I hopped out of my chair, ready for my big *Crocodile Dundee* moment—if only I could figure out how to go about fighting without fists.

I mean, they don't call it a "shoulder fight," do they?

The lunchtime crowd ringed around us as Chucky and I circled each other. I was still thinking that he wouldn't possibly go through with it. Who would be so low as to hit a little kid with no arms and no legs?

Girls in my class were crying, "Nicky, don't do it. He'll hurt you."

That got to me. I didn't want girl pity. My macho pride kicked in. I walked right up to Chucky like I knew I could kick his butt.

He gave me a double stiff arm to the chest, and I went backward arse over earlobes, flopping onto the concrete like a sack of potatoes.

Chucky had gobsmacked me! I'd never been knocked down like that. *It hurt!* But the embarrassment was far worse. My schoolmates huddled over me, horrified. Girls cried out, shielding their eyes from what they thought was a pitiful sight.

This bloke is really trying to hurt me, I realized. I flipped over and pressed my forehead to the ground. Then I leveraged a shoulder against my wheelchair to get myself upright. This technique made for a calloused forehead and a very strong neck, qualities that would soon spell Chucky's downfall.

I had no doubt: Chucky had no qualms about kicking my butt. It was fight or flight, and flight wasn't a realistic option.

I charged Chucky again, with a bit more speed behind me this time. Three hops, and I was right in front of him. But before I could think what to do next, Chucky nailed me with a straight arm. Just one arm *bam* to the chest, and I slammed to the ground. I even bounced once. Okay, maybe twice.

My head conked on the hard-hearted Oval. The world faded to black. A shrieking girl quickly brought me back to my senses.

I prayed for the teacher cavalry. Why can you never find an assistant principal when you need one?

Finally my vision cleared, and there was the evil Chucky hovering over me. The fat-faced mongrel was doing a victory dance.

That does it. I'm laying this bloke out!

I flipped onto my stomach, planted my forehead, and raised myself up for a final charge. My adrenaline was pumping. This time I galloped at him as fast as I could go, which was a lot faster than Chucky had anticipated.

He'd started to backpedal on his knees. I took a flying leap, using my left foot to launch myself like a human missile. My flying head butted Chucky smack in the nose. He went down. I landed on top of him and rolled.

When I looked up, Chucky was sprawled on the ground, holding his nose and bawling uncontrollably.

Instead of feeling victorious, I was overcome by guilt. The pastor's son begged for forgiveness: "I'm so sorry, are you okay?"

"Look, Chucky's bleeding!" a girl cried.

No way, I thought.

But sure enough, blood from Chucky's nose was leaking through his pudgy fingers. He took his hand away, and it poured down his face and stained his shirt in bright red.

Half the crowd was cheering. The other half was mortified—for Chucky. After all, he'd just been beat up by a shrimp with no arms or legs. He would never live this down. Chucky's bullying days were over. He pinched his nose with his fingers and scurried into the bathroom.

Honestly, I never saw him again. He must have quit school in shame. Chucky, if you are out there, I'm sorry, and I hope you have had a good post-bully life.

I was proud of sticking up for myself but burdened by guilt. After school I went home and confessed to my parents as soon as I walked in the door. I was dreading a severe punishment. But I had no need to be worried. Dad and mum didn't believe me! They simply did not think it possible that I'd beaten up a bigger, older, and fully-equipped bloke!

I didn't try to convince them otherwise.

As much as people enjoy hearing this story and as funny as certain aspects of it are, I have mixed feelings about even telling it, since I don't advocate violence. I believe meekness is strength withheld. I'll always remember my first—and only—fight because I discovered that when push came to shove, I could overcome my fears. At that age especially, it felt good to know that I had the strength to defend myself. I guess you could say I learned that I could afford to be meek because I had tapped the strength inside me.

NO ARMS, NO LEGS, NO FEAR

You may have a strong sense of purpose, great hope for the possibilities in your life, faith in your future, an appreciation for your own value, and even a great attitude, but fear can hold you back from achieving your dreams. There are many handicaps worse than having no arms and no legs—fear can be especially debilitating. You cannot live a fulfilling life that fully expresses your blessings if fear controls your every decision.

Fear will hold you back and keep you from being who you want to be. But fear is just a mood, a feeling—it's not real! How often have you feared something—a trip to the dentist, a job interview, an operation, or a test in school—only to discover that the actual experience was not nearly as bad as you had imagined?

I thought I would get creamed in my first-grade fight with Chucky-boy, but look how that turned out! All too often adults revert back to childish fears. They go back to acting like kids frightened at night because they imagine that the tree limb scraping the bedroom window is actually a monster trying to eat them up.

That was some good chocolate! Thanks, Mum!

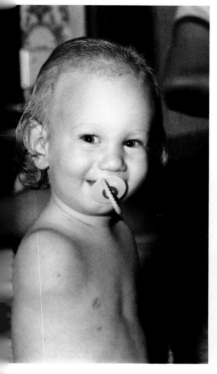

This is my favorite photo (6 months old). Happy, confident, and cute—right? My blissful ignorance was a blessing at that age, not knowing that I was different or that many challenges awaited me.

At 2½, driving and getting acquainted with my first set of wheels. Watch your feet, guys!

Always one of my favorite places to go and play with my favorite cars and trucks. I loved the sand in sunny Queensland, and at 3, I'd jump the ripples of the little waves on the shore.

My brother's and my favorite game to play was Battleship. I sometimes used my arms but in the end it was clear that I managed to accomplish most tasks more efficiently on my own without the aid of prosthetics.

As Joni Eareckson-Tada said, "We've all got wheels." I feel a sense of liberation when using my custom-built electronic wheelchair. *(photo courtesy of Ally)*

Mission accomplished: I graduated a double-major at Griffith University with a Bachelor of Commerce in Financial Planning and Accounting in 2003 at the age of 21.

Me with Mum and Dad (Dushka and Boris) at the Anaheim
Angel Stadium before I went onstage in front of 55,000 people
in 2009.

Hangin' with my brother, Aaron, and his wife, Michelle.

Soaking up the summer and catching up with my beautiful sister, Michelle.

orking out hand signals with my instructor as I go scuba-diving in a pool for the
st time to get a feel for it. Cool experience!

My amazing experience surfing with Bethany Hamilton in Hawaii. She was gracious in giving me a tandem ride while I searched for the courage to find my balance on my own. *(Photo courtesy of NoahHamiltonPhoto.com)*

And the beach goes wild! *(Photo courtesy of NoahHamiltonPhoto.com)*

ms sweating
ht before a large
ngregation in Ghana!

Wherever I travel around the world, I try to encourage whoever I meet that they can overcome adversity with faith, hope, love, and courage so that they may pursue their dreams. The joy of these boys lifted me up and I'll never forget the time we had in South Africa in 2002.

still excites me to get
front of any crowd,
ywhere, of any size
be with kids, play,
d just be! Being with
ildren helps me stay
wn-to-earth, especially
ds from Colombia who
e to play soccer!
hoto courtesy of Carlos
rgara)

I've had the honor of meeting ma[ny]
inspirational people who have lef[t]
me breathless. I'll never forget ho[w]
Jeanette encouraged and inspired
all that were blessed to know her[.]
Some would say that she lost her
fight to cancer, but I'll say her
loving Heavenly Daddy carried h[er]
tired body home. She lost nothin[g]
and she left us broken-hearted, ye[t]
she let us see how strength can b[e]
perfected in weakness.
(Photo courtesy of Tony Cruz)

HERE WE GO!

I've seen fear absolutely paralyze otherwise normal people. I'm not referring to scary movie fears or childhood fears of bumps in the night. So many people are handicapped by fear of failure, fear of making mistakes, fear of making a commitment, even fear of success. It's inevitable that fears will come knocking on your door. You don't have to let them in. You send them on their way, and then go on yours. You have that choice.

Psychologists say most fears are learned. We are born with only two instinctive fears: fear of loud noises and fear of being dropped. I had a fear of being mauled by Chucky back in the first grade, but I got over it. I decided that I wasn't going to wait until I felt brave—I just acted brave, and in the end I *was* brave!

Even as adults we create fearful fantasies that simply don't match up to reality. This explains why fear is often described as "**F**alse **E**vidence **A**ppearing **R**eal." We become so focused on our fears that they become real to us—and as a result, we let them control us.

It's hard to imagine someone as big and successful as Michael Jordan being afraid. Yet during his induction into the NBA Hall of Fame, Jordan talked openly about how he often used his fears to drive himself to be a better athlete. At the conclusion of his speech, he said, "One day you might look up and see me playing the game at fifty. Oh, don't laugh, don't laugh. Never say never. Because limits, like fears, are often just an illusion."

Jordan may have been a better basketball player than life coach, but he had a point. Follow the Jordan rules; recognize that fears are not real and soar past them, or put them to use. The key to dealing with your worst fears, whether it is fear of flying, fear of failing, or fear of relationships, is to recognize that the fear is not real. It is an emotion, and you can control your response to your emotions.

I had to learn this lesson early in my speaking career. I was very fearful and nervous. I did not know how people would respond to what I had to say. I wasn't sure they'd even listen to me. Fortunately, my first speaking engagements were to my fellow students. They knew me, and we were comfortable with each other. Over time I began speaking to larger youth groups and churches with only a few friends sprinkled into the crowd. Gradually I overcame my nervousness and fears.

I still experience fear when I am called to speak to many thousands of people, sometimes tens and hundreds of thousands. I go into remote areas of China, South America, Africa, and other parts of the world where I have no idea how people will receive me. I'm afraid I'll tell a joke that means something entirely different in their culture and they'll take offense. I use that fear to remind myself to always run my speeches by my interpreters and hosts before I risk embarrassment.

I've learned to welcome my fear as a source of energy and as a tool to focus my preparations. If I'm afraid of forgetting my speech or messing something up, it helps me concentrate on reviewing and practicing my presentation.

Many fears are useful in that way. For example, it is a good fear that motivates you to snap on the seat belt because you don't want to be injured in a car accident. If your fear of catching a cold or a flu inspires you to wash your hands and take vitamins, that's good too.

Too often, though, we allow our learned fears to run amok. Instead of simply taking precautions to avoid catching a flu or cold, some people take it to an extreme by locking themselves in their homes and refusing to go outdoors. When our fears keep us from doing all we can do or from being all we can be, they are not reasonable.

"WHAT IF?" FEARS

I have a friend whose parents divorced when she was young. Her mum and dad fought all the time, even after they broke up. Now she is a grown woman, but she is afraid to get married. "I don't want to end up like my parents," she says.

Can you imagine never having a lasting relationship because you are afraid it might not work out? That's a sick fear! You can't think of marriage as nothing but the first step to divorce. Remember the Tennyson poem " 'Tis better to have loved and lost than never to have loved at all"?

You can't possibly have an enjoyable and fulfilling life if you are paralyzed by fear of what might happen someday, somewhere, maybe, somehow. If we all stayed in our beds every day because we were afraid of being struck by lightning or bitten by a malaria mosquito, it would be a pretty sad world, wouldn't it?

So many fearful people focus on the *What if* when they should be saying *Why not!*

- *What if I fail!*

- *What if I'm not good enough!*

- *What if they laugh at me!*

- *What if I'm turned down!*

- *What if I can't keep up with my successes!*

I understand that sort of thinking. Growing up I had to deal with major fears—the fear of rejection, the fear of inadequacy, the fear of being dependent. It wasn't just my imagination: my body lacked the standard equipment. But my parents told me that I should always focus not on what was missing but on what I had and what I could create if I only dared to follow my imagination.

"Dream big, Nicky, and never let fear keep you from working toward your dreams," they said. "You can't let fear dictate your future. Choose the life you want and go for it."

So far, I've spoken to diverse audiences in more than nineteen countries around the globe. I've taken my message of hope and faith to vast crowds in stadiums, arenas, schools, churches, and prisons. I never could have done that if my parents had not encouraged me to acknowledge my fears and then push past them.

FEAR AS MOTIVATION

You and I will never be as dominant in a sport as Michael Jordan was, but you can be like Mike in using fear as a motivational tool to keep chasing your dreams and the life you want to create.

Laura Gregory was a very smart school friend. I could always count on her to say exactly what she was thinking. She did not mess around. One day in our first year, Laura asked, "So you have a teacher's aide to help you at school. But who takes care of you at home?"

"Well, my parents do," I said, though I wasn't certain what she was getting at.

"Are you okay with that?"

"With my parents helping me? Sure, what else would I do?"

"I mean with things like getting dressed and showering and using the bathroom?" she said. "What about your dignity? Don't you think it's a little weird that you can't do that on your own?"

Laura didn't mean to hurt my feelings. She was a truth seeker, and she truly wanted to know how I felt about every aspect of my life. But she touched on a sensitive subject. One of my greatest fears growing up was that I was a burden on the people I loved. The thought of being overly dependent on my parents, and on my brother and sister too, was never far from my mind. Sometimes I would wake up at night in a cold sweat, terrorized by the thought of my parents being gone, leaving me dependent on Aaron or Michelle.

That fear was a very real one. Sometimes I was nearly overwhelmed by visions of dependency. Laura's blunt questions about my dignity helped move me from being *tormented* by that fear to being *motivated* by it. Questions about my dependency had always lingered on the edges of my consciousness, but after that day I put them at the forefront of my mind, and I decided to address them aggressively.

If I really put my mind to it, just how independent could I become? Motivated by my fear of burdening my loved ones, I created that mission statement—even though at the time I had not a clue as to what a mission statement was. My fear gave me a driving passion and the strength to push myself. *I need to do more for myself. But how?*

My parents always assured me that they were there to help me and that they didn't mind carrying me, lifting me, dressing me, or doing whatever I needed them to do. But it bothered me that I couldn't even get a drink of water by myself, and someone always had to lift me onto the toilet seat. As I grew older, I naturally wanted more independence, and I wanted to look after myself more. My fear gave me the determination to take action on those desires.

One of the thoughts that really stirred me to action was the image of me being a burden on my brother Aaron once my parents were no longer around. I'd often worried about that because if anybody deserved a normal life, it was my poor little brother. I felt like God owed him that because for most of his life he'd been stuck helping me, living with me, and seeing me get so much attention. Aaron had arms and legs, but in some ways he got the raw end of the deal because he always felt he had to look out for me.

My decision to become more self-sufficient, as much as any concern, was a matter of self-preservation. Laura reminded me that I was still dependent on the kindness and patience of others. I knew that I could not always be so reliant on that. And pride played into it too.

I am fully capable of having a family one day, and I would never want my wife to have to carry me around. I want to have kids and be a good father and a good provider too, so I thought, *I need to get out of this wheelchair.*

Fear can be your foe, but in this case I made it my friend. I announced to my parents that I wanted to find ways to care for myself. They were, of course, worried at first.

"You don't have to do that. We'll make sure you're always cared for," they said.

"Mum, Dad, I must do this for you and for me, so let's put our heads together and figure this out," I said.

And we did. In some ways our creative efforts reminded me of the old *Swiss Family Robinson* movie. Stranded on an island, they all pitch in and devise amazing gadgets for bathing, cooking, and surviving. I know no man is an island, especially a man with no arms and no legs. Maybe I was more like a peninsula, or an isthmus.

My mum the nurse and my dad the handyman first came up with a method for me to shower and shampoo my hair. Dad replaced the round knobs on the shower with levers that I could move with my shoulders. Then mum brought home a hands-free soap dispenser with a foot pump, used by doctors prepping for surgery. We adapted it so I could use it to pump soap and shampoo by stepping on it.

Then my dad and I came up with a design for a plastic holder to mount on the wall for an electric toothbrush. I could turn it on and off by pressing a switch and then brush my teeth by moving back and forth.

I told my parents that I wanted to be able to dress myself, so my mum made shorts with a Velcro strip that I could slip in and out of by myself. Shirt buttons have always been a challenge for me, so we found shirts that I could slip on and off by throwing them over my head and wriggling into them.

My major fear had sent the three of us on a mission that was both challenging and fun as we invented ways for me to be more independent. Remote controls, cell phones, computer keyboards, and remote garage-door openers are a blessing for me because I can operate them with my foot.

Some of the solutions we came up with weren't exactly high tech. I learned how to turn off our home security alarm using my nose to push the buttons, and I used a golf club wedged between my chin and neck to turn on the lights and open some of the windows in the house.

I won't go into great detail on it, for obvious reasons, but we also devised some ingenious methods that allowed me to use the restroom by myself. You can see some of our methods and devices on this YouTube video: http://www.youtube.com/watch?v=0DxlJWJ_WfA. Be assured, there is no restroom footage.

I am thankful for Laura's little talk with me about my dignity, and I'm thankful for my youthful fear of being dependent and a burden on my family because it motivated me to become more independent. Mastering even routine tasks that others take for granted did wonders for my self-confidence, but I might never have pushed myself to do it if not for some potentially negative emotions that I turned into positive energy.

You can do the same. Tap the energy generated by your fears of failure or rejection or similar fears, and use it to power positive action that puts you closer to your dream.

FEAR FRAMED

You can also counter fears that might paralyze you by fighting them with fear itself. Think of your biggest fear. Let's say it's a fear of getting up in front of a huge audience and forgetting your speech. That's one I can identify with. Go ahead, visualize the very worst happening: you forget your speech and they boo you off the stage. Got that image? Okay. Next, visualize yourself giving your speech so well that the audience gives you a standing ovation.

Now, make the choice to go with the second scenario and lock it into your mind so that every time you prepare to speak, you move past your fear of the *boos* and go right to the standing ovation. It works for me, and it can work for you.

A similar method for moving beyond a fear is to go back to your memory file of real-life experiences in which you have persevered and overcome challenges. For example, when I feel fearful and nervous about meeting an important person such as Oprah Winfrey, I just tap my memory bank for a shot of courage.

You're scared to meet Oprah! What's she going to do, cut off your arms and legs! Wait, you've already lived more than twenty-five years and traveled the world without arms and legs. Oprah, I'm ready for you! Give me a hug!

STUCK WITH FEAR

When I was a kid, I had what seemed like a very natural fear, a fear of doctors with needles. Whenever I had to get my school vaccinations for measles and rubella or the flu, I'd hide from my mum. Part of the problem was that doctors had a limited number of places on my body where they could stick me. With other kids, they could do either arm or the butt. My abbreviated body offered only one target site, and since my bum sits very low to the ground, it was especially painful for me, even when they administered the shot high in my hip. Whenever I received a shot, I couldn't walk for a day.

Because of my disability, I'd spent a good part of my youth serving as a pincushion for doctors with needles, and I'd developed a very deep fear. I was known for fainting at the mere sight of a hypodermic and syringe.

Once in grade school, two school nurses who apparently didn't know either my history or much about human anatomy came up on either side of me, pinned me between them in my wheelchair, and gave me shots in both shoulders—where there is very little muscle or fat. It was excruciating. The pain was so bad, I asked my friend Jerry to walk alongside me and steer my wheelchair because I felt faint. Jerry took control, and sure enough, I blacked out. Poor Jerry didn't know what to do, so he steered my wheelchair into our science class, with me hanging over the side, and asked the teacher for help.

Knowing my great fear of needles, my mum didn't tell me or my brother or sister that we were headed to the doctor for our school inoculations. When I was about twelve years old, we had a wild visit that became part of family lore. Mum claimed we were just going in for our school "checkups." My first tip-off was in the waiting room. We'd seen this little girl about my age go into the examining area, and then we heard her screaming as she received her shot.

"Did you hear that?" I asked Aaron and Michelle. "They are giving us the needle too!"

My fear kicked in, and I went into a panic. I was crying and yelling, telling my mum that I didn't want to get a shot, that they hurt too much and I wanted to go home. Since I was the oldest child, the younger kids followed my brave and shining example. They too started caterwauling and begging to go home.

Our mother the nurse had no sympathy, of course. She was a veteran of the hypodermic wars. She hauled her howling and kicking and clawing pack into the examining room like a marine MP dragging drunken soldiers to the brig.

Seeing that sheer panic and pitiful begging was not working, I tried negotiation with the family physician. "Don't you just have something I can drink instead?" I bawled.

"I'm afraid not, my son."

Time for Plan B, as in Brother. I turned to Aaron and asked him to help me escape. I had a getaway all planned out. Aaron was to distract the doctors by falling off the examining table so I could squirm out of my wheelchair and make a run for it. But mum intercepted me. Ever the opportunist, my little sister bolted for the door. A passing nurse grabbed her in the hallway, but then Michelle wedged her little arms and legs in the doorway so they couldn't get her into the examining room. She was my hero!

Our hysterical cries could be heard throughout the clinic. Staff came running because it sounded as though we were being brutally tortured. Unfortunately, the reinforcements quickly took the wrong side. Two of them pinned me down for an injection. I screamed like a banshee.

I kept squirming just as they went to jam the needle in my bum. I jerked around and forced the needle to go in and pop out again. So the doctor had to jam it in me again! My screams set off car alarms in the parking lot.

How any of us—my siblings, my mother, or the clinic staff—survived that day, I'll never know. The three of us wailed all the way home.

Because I was so afraid, my fears made the pain worse than it would have been if I'd just let them administer the shot. In fact, I doubled my pain because I did not manage my fear. I couldn't walk for two days instead of just one!

So keep that little fable from my life in mind: when you let your fears control your actions, you are only asking for serious pain in your bum!

SEVEN

Don't Let Your Face Plant Grow Roots

As you might imagine, I had a long black-and-blue history of falls and face plants as a child. I toppled off tables, high chairs, beds, stairs, and ramps. Lacking arms to break my fall, I usually took it on the chin, not to mention the nose and forehead. I've gone down hard many times.

What I've never done is stay down. There is a Japanese proverb that describes my formula for success: "Fall seven times, stand up eight."

You fail. I fail. The best of us fail, and the rest of us fail too. Those who never rise from defeat often see failure as final. What we all need to remember is that life is not a pass-fail test. It's a trial-and-error process. Those who succeed bounce back from their bonehead mistakes because they view their setbacks as temporary and as learning experiences. Every successful person I know has messed up at some point. Often, they say their mistakes were critical to their success. When they flopped, they didn't quit. Instead, they recognized their problems, worked harder, and searched for more creative solutions. If they failed five times, they tried five times harder. Winston Churchill captured the essence of it when he said, "Success is the ability to go from one failure to another with no loss of enthusiasm."

If you can't overcome your defeats, it may be that you have personalized them. Losing doesn't make you a loser any more than striking out makes a great baseball player a benchwarmer. As long as you stay in the game and keep swinging, you can still be a slugger. If you aren't willing to do the work required, then losing isn't your problem, you are the problem. To achieve success you have to feel worthy of it and then take responsibility for making it happen.

In my speeches, I demonstrate my philosophy on failure by flopping down on my belly and continuing to talk to the audience from that position. Given my lack of limbs, you might think that it would be impossible for me to get up on my own. My audiences often think that too.

My parents say I taught myself to rise up from a horizontal position as a toddler. They'd put pillows down and coax me to brace against them. But I had to do it my way, the hard way, of course. Instead of using the pillows, I'd crawl to a wall or a chair or couch, wedge my forehead against it to get leverage, then inch myself up.

It's not the easiest thing to do. Try it if you like. Get on the floor on your stomach and try to rise to your knees without using your arms or legs for leverage. You don't feel very graceful, do you? But what feels better, rising up or staying down? That's because you weren't made to wallow on the ground. You were made to rise again and again and again until you have fully unleashed your potential.

Now and then when I demonstrate my rising technique in my speeches, I'll run into a glitch of some sort. I usually speak from an elevated platform, a stage or even a desk or tabletop if we're in a classroom or a conference room. At one school appearance, I flopped down before I realized that someone with good intentions had spray-waxed the top of the table before my speech. It was slicker than an Olympic ice rink up there. I tried to rub a spot clean of the spray wax so I could get a grip, but no luck. It was a bit embarrassing when I had to give up on the lesson and call for help: "Could someone please give me a hand?"

On another occasion, I was speaking at a fundraiser in Houston to a large and distinguished audience, including Jeb Bush, the former governor of Florida, and his wife, Columba. As I prepared to talk about the importance of never giving up, I went down on my belly, as usual. The crowd fell silent, as usual.

"We all fail from time to time," I said. "But failing is like falling. You just have to keep getting back up, never giving up on your dreams."

The audience was really into it, but before I could demonstrate that even I have the ability to rise again, this woman I'd never met came scurrying up from the back of the room.

"Here, let me help you up," she said.

"But I don't need any help," I whispered through gritted teeth. "This is part of my speech."

"Don't be silly. Let me help you," she insisted.

"Ma'am, please, I really don't need your help. I'm trying to make a point."

"Well, okay then, if you are sure, sweetie," she said before returning to her seat.

I think the audience was nearly as relieved to see her sit down as they were to see me get up! People often get emotional when they see what it takes for me to simply lift myself up from the floor. They relate to my struggle because we all struggle. You can take heart in that too when your plans hit a wall or hard times hit you. Your trials and tribulations are a part of life shared by the rest of humanity.

Even if you create a sense of purpose for your life, keep hoping for the possibilities, have faith in your future, appreciate your value, maintain a positive attitude, and refuse to let your fears hold you back, you will endure setbacks and disappointments. You should never think of failures as final, never equate them with death or dying, because the reality is that in your struggles you are experiencing life. You are in the game. The challenges we face can help make us stronger, better, and more prepared for success.

THE LESSONS OF LOSING

You could view your failures as a gift because they often set you up for a breakthrough. So what benefits can be derived in defeat or setbacks? I can think of at least four valuable lessons failure gives us.

1. It is a great teacher.
2. It builds character.
3. It motivates you.
4. It helps you appreciate success.

It is a great teacher

Yes, defeat is a great teacher. Every winner has played the loser. Every champion has been the runner-up. Roger Federer is considered one of the best tennis players of all time, but he doesn't win every game, set, or match. He hits bad shots into the net. He slams serves out of bounds. He fails to place the tennis ball where he wants it dozens of times in every match. If Roger gave up after every failed shot, he'd be a failure. Instead, he learns from his misses and his losses and stays in the game. That's why he is a champion.

Does Federer always *try* to hit the perfect shot and to win every game, set, and match? Certainly, and so should you in whatever you do. Work hard. Practice. Master the fundamentals, and always try to do your best, knowing that sometimes you will fail because failure is on the path to mastery.

My younger brother teases me about my early years of developing as a speaker when I often failed to find an audience. I'd beg schools and organizations for the chance to speak to them, but most turned me down as too young or too inexperienced or just too unusual. It was frustrating sometimes, but I knew I was still learning the ropes, figuring out what I needed to know to be a successful speaker.

When Aaron was in high school, he'd drive me all over the city searching for even a few people willing to listen to me. I'd speak for free just for the experience. Even then my price was often too high. I must have rung up every school in Brisbane offering my services at no charge. Most turned me down initially, but every *no* just made me push harder for the next *yes*.

"Don't you ever give up?" Aaron would say.

I didn't give up because every time I was turned down it hurt so much that I realized I'd found my passion. I really wanted to become a speaker. But even when I did manage to find an audience willing to listen to me, it didn't always go well. At one school in Brisbane, I started badly. Something distracted me, and I couldn't find my way back on track. I was sweating through my shirt. I kept repeating myself. I wanted to crawl off in a hole and never be seen again. I did so poorly I thought word would spread and I'd never be asked to speak in public for the rest of my life. When I finally finished and left the school, I felt like a laughingstock: my reputation was shot!

We can be our own harshest critics. I certainly was that day. But that flubbed performance made me focus even more on my dream. I worked at honing my presentation and delivery. Once you accept that perfection is just a goal, screwing up isn't so hard to handle. Each misstep is still a step, another lesson learned, another opportunity to get it right the next time.

I realized that if you fail and give up, you will never get up. But if you learn the lessons of failure and keep trying to do your best, the rewards will come—not just in the approval of others but in the fulfillment of knowing that you are making the most of every day allotted to you.

It builds character

Is it possible that messing up can build you up and make you more fit for success? Yes! What does not destroy you can make you stronger, more focused, more creative, and more determined to pursue your dreams. You may be in a rush to succeed, and there is nothing wrong with that, but patience is a virtue too, and failure certainly will develop that trait in you. Believe me, I've learned that my schedule isn't necessarily in God's day planner. He has His own time line and the rest of us have to wait for it to unfold.

This lesson really hit me when I joined my uncle Sam Radojevic in a startup business to manufacture and market his recumbent bicycle called the Hippo Cycle. We began in 2006, and our company still hasn't taken off, but with each setback and mistake, we learn a little more and move a little closer to our goal. We are building a business and our characters too, no doubt about that. I've learned that sometimes even though you may be doing your best, it's not enough to make a business work. Timing can be critical too. The economy suffered a recession just as we launched the business. We've had to be patient, hang in there, and wait for the times and the trends to come back our way.

There will be times when you will have to wait for the world to catch up to you. Thomas Edison, who went through more than ten thousand failed experiments before he developed a commercial lightbulb, said most of those who consider themselves failures are people who did not realize how close to success they were when they gave up. They were almost there, going through failure, but still bound for success. But they gave up before the tide could turn for them.

You never know what lies around the next corner. It could be the answer to your dreams. So you have to buck up, stay strong, and keep fighting. If you fail, so what? If you fall, so what? Edison also said: "Every wrong attempt discarded is another step forward."

If you do your best, God will do the rest, and whatever is meant to come your way will come. You have to be strong of character to win, and every loss can be a character-building experience if you are open to it.

In 2009 I spoke at the Oaks Christian School in Westlake, California. This small school is known for being a giant killer on the football field. Just recently their starting quarterback was the son of famed NFL quarterback Joe Montana. His backup was the son of Wayne Gretzky, the hockey legend. And their star receiver was the son of the wonderful actor Will Smith.

Their football team has won six consecutive conference championships. When I spoke there, I met the founder of the school, David Price, and I realized where Oaks Christian athletic teams learned about strength of character.

David had been an attorney in a big Hollywood law firm with movie stars and movie studios as clients. He then went to work for an entrepreneur who owned hotels and resorts along with land all over California, including several golf courses. David was adept at managing businesses, and he saw that most golf courses were poorly run because they were usually operated by golf professionals who had never learned good business practices.

One day David went to his boss and said he wanted to buy a golf course from him.

"First of all, you work for me," the boss said, "so why should I sell you anything? Secondly, you know nothing about golf. And thirdly, you have no money!"

David failed to convince his boss at first, but he didn't give up. He persevered. He kept pestering him until the boss bought into David's dream and sold him the golf course he wanted. It was just the first of more than 350 golf courses that David eventually owned or leased.

Then when the golf course business suffered a downturn, David sold out. Now he buys, leases, and manages airports around the country. What did David learn from failure? Patience and perseverance, for sure. He never gave up on his dream. When the market dropped in the golf business, David also took stock and realized that his real skill wasn't managing golf courses, it was managing businesses. So he simply transferred that skill over to another arena.

David, who is now on the board of my Life Without Limbs nonprofit organization, told me the bigger the challenges we endure, the greater our strength of character. "Nick, if you'd been born with arms and legs, I don't think you would be as successful as you will become without them one day," David said. "How many kids would listen to you if they couldn't see right away that you have turned what should have been an incredible negative into something so positive?"

Remember those words when you experience challenges. For every blocked path, there is an open one. For every "disability," there is an ability. You were put on this earth to serve a purpose, so don't ever let a loss convince you that there are no ways to win. As long as you draw breath with the rest of us mortals, there is always a way.

I'm grateful that I've failed and persevered. My challenges made me more patient and more tenacious too. Those traits have come in handy in my work and in my play. One of my favorite ways to relax is to go fishing. My parents first took me when I was just six years old. They'd stick my pole in the ground or in a holder until I got a bite. Then I'd tuck my chin around the pole and hold on to the fish until someone could come and help me.

On one day I wasn't having much luck, but I hung in there, watching my line for three hours straight. The sun roasted me to a crispy crimson, but I was determined to catch a fish that day. My parents had wandered off, fishing down the shoreline, so I was alone when a fish finally hit my bait. I stomped my hand line with my toes and screamed "Mum! Dad!" until they came running.

When they pulled it in, that fish was twice my size. But I never would have landed him if I hadn't hung in there and refused to let go with my toe.

Of course, failure can also build humility into your character. I failed in my high school accounting class, which was a humbling experience. I was afraid that maybe I didn't have what it took to be a numbers cruncher, but my teacher encouraged me and tutored me. I studied and studied, and years later I earned a double degree in accounting and financial planning.

I needed that lesson in humility when I was a student. I needed to fail so I could learn that I didn't know all I needed to know. In the end, humility made me stronger. The writer Thomas Merton said, "A humble man is not afraid of failure. In fact, he is not afraid of anything, even of himself, since perfect humility implies perfect confidence in the power of God before Whom no other power has any meaning and for Whom there is no such thing as an obstacle."

It motivates you

We can choose to respond to loss or failure by despairing and giving up, or we can let the loss or failure serve as a learning experience and motivation to do better. A friend of mine is a fitness instructor, and I've heard him tell clients who are bench-pressing weights to "go to failure." Now that's encouraging, isn't it? But the theory is that you keep pumping the iron until your muscles are exhausted so that next time you can try to exceed that limit and build more strength.

One of the keys to success in any sport and in your work too is practice. I think of practice as failing toward success, and I can give you a perfect example that involves me and my cell phone. You may think the smart phone is a great invention, but for me it is a gift from heaven. Sometimes I think the inventors must have had me in mind when they created a single device that even a guy without arms or legs can use to talk on the telephone, send e-mails, text messages, play music, tape-record sermons and memos, and keep up with the weather and world events just by tapping it with my toes.

The smart phone isn't quite perfectly designed for me since the only part of me that can use the touch screen is a long way from the part of me that can talk! I can use the speaker feature most of the time, but when I'm in an airport or a restaurant, I don't want to share my conversations with everyone around me.

I had to figure out a way to position my cell phone closer to my mouth once I'd dialed it with my foot. The method I devised gives new meaning to the term "flip phone" and offers a bruising lesson in the role of failure in success. I spent a good week trying to use my little foot to flip my phone onto my shoulder, where I'd pin it down with my chin so I could talk on it. (Kids, don't try this at home!) During this trial-and-error period, you can believe I failed in many attempts. My face had so many bruises from getting hit by the phone that I looked like I'd been smacked with a bag full of nickels.

I only practiced when no one was around, because if someone had seen me, they might have thought I was into cellular self-abuse. I won't tell you how many times I whacked myself in the head or nose with my cell phone—or how many cell phones died in the mastery of the task. I could afford to take a few hits and to replace a few cell phones. What I couldn't afford to do was give up.

Every time that cell phone cracked me in the face, I became more and more motivated to master the feat, and eventually I did! Of course, as fate would have it, shortly after I finally mastered the skill, the tech world came out with Bluetooth headsets that rest in your ear. Now my famous cell-phone flip is a relic of technology past and it's just something I do to entertain friends when they're bored.

I encourage you to look at your own setbacks and pratfalls as sources of motivation and inspiration. There's no shame in falling short, striking out, tripping up, or screwing up. It's only a shame if you don't use the motivation from your misses and miscues to try harder and stay in the game.

It helps you appreciate success

The fourth gift of failure is that it serves as success appreciation class. Believe me, after a week of being whapped by my bad cell-phone flips, I felt enormous appreciation when I finally nailed the landing on my shoulder. In fact, the harder you have to work to achieve a goal, the more you will appreciate it. How many times have you looked back from a big victory and thought how sweet it was to finally triumph after your long struggle? Admit it, the tougher the climb, the better the view at the top.

One of my favorite childhood Bible stories was that of Joseph, the favored but proud son whose jealous brothers sold him into slavery. Joseph had a rough go for a long time. He was falsely accused of a crime, thrown into prison, and betrayed time and again by people he trusted. But Joseph didn't give up. He didn't let bitterness or failure defeat him. He persevered to become the ruler of Egypt who saved his people.

There are many lessons to draw from Joseph's struggles and his ultimate ascension to the throne. One I learned is that success may not come without pain. Joseph's trials helped me understand that while my life certainly seemed harder than most, others suffered more yet endured and achieved greatness. I saw that while God loves us, He makes no promises that life will be easy. And finally, I saw that once Joseph emerged from his many trials and betrayals, he savored his triumph by becoming a great and just king.

When you put your whole heart into achieving a goal and you go through great pain and suffering along the way, the feeling of achievement once you break through is so incredible that you just want to build on it, don't you? I don't think that is an accident. It may be one of the main reasons humankind has come so far. We celebrate tough victories not because we survived the effort but because our nature is to keep growing and seeking even higher levels of fulfillment.

In those times when God makes me work harder and harder for my goals, putting one stumbling block after another in my path, I truly believe that He is preparing me for bigger and better days. He throws challenges at us because He knows that when we go through failure, we grow.

Looking back at all I had to overcome at such a young age—the pain, the insecurity, the hurt, the loneliness—I don't feel sad. I feel humbled and grateful because I overcame those challenges that make my successes all the sweeter. In the end, they made me stronger, and, more important, they made me better equipped to reach out to others. Without my pain I would never be able to help anybody else deal with their pain. I wouldn't be able to relate so well with other people. As I approached my teen years, the knowledge of what I'd overcome made me more confident. That new level of self-confidence, in turn, attracted other kids to me. I formed a big circle of male and female friends. I loved the attention! I'd wheel around school basking in the warmth.

Of course, you know where that led—to politics. I summoned the courage to run for the school captain—which was the presidency of the entire student body of twelve hundred kids at Mac-Gregor State School, which was like a combined junior high and high school and one of the largest schools in Queensland.

Not only was I the first physically disabled kid to run for school captain, I was running against one of the best athletes in the school's history—Matthew McKay, who is now a famous soccer player in Australia. My teacher, Mrs. Hurley, encouraged me to run after I was surprised to be nominated by my classmates. I ran on a platform of diversity and multiculturalism, and my campaign promise was to hold wheelchair races on school sports day.

I won in a landslide (sorry Matthew). My mum still has a clip from the *Courier-Mail* newspaper, which featured a big photograph and story with a headline hailing me as "Captain Courageous."

The same newspaper quoted me as saying: "All wheelchair kids, I reckon, should just give everything a go."

My boyhood slogan may not be as recognized as Nike's "Just Do It!" but it served me well. You will fail because you are human. You will fall because the path is rough. But know that your failures too are part of the gift of life, so put them to their highest use. Don't stop, mate. Give everything a go!

EIGHT

The New Bloke in the Bushes

I was twelve years old when my family moved from Australia to the United States. I was scared out of my wits to be starting all over in a place where I had no friends. On the plane to our new country, my brother and little sister and I practiced our American accents so we wouldn't be teased when we talked to our new schoolmates.

I couldn't do anything about my unusual body, but I figured I could fix my foreign accent. Later I learned that most Americans love Australian accents. *Crocodile Dundee* had been a big hit just a few years earlier. By trying to sound like my classmates, I missed out on all sorts of opportunities to impress girls.

This was the first major change in my life, and trying to sound American wasn't the only mistake I made. My new school was Lindero Canyon Middle School, which is in the foothills of the Santa Monica Mountains not far from where I live today. It was a wonderful school but I struggled there at first. It's hard for any kid to move away from where he's grown up, switch schools, and make new friends. Along with the usual hurdles of being new, I didn't look like a "normal" kid. I was the only student in a wheelchair, and the only one with a teacher's aide. Most teens worry that they'll be made fun of if they have a pimple. Imagine my concern.

I'd already fought to be accepted back in Australia, in my first school in Melbourne and then again when we moved to the Brisbane area. It took so much energy to convince my classmates that I was cool enough to hang out with. Now I was forced to begin anew.

CHANGE U.

Sometimes when we go through transitions, we aren't aware of the impact they have on us. Stress, doubt, and even depression commonly result from being moved or thrown out of your comfort zone, however easy the transition is. You may have a strong sense of purpose, high hopes, strong faith, a powerful sense of self-worth, a positive attitude, the courage to face your fears, and the ability to bounce back from failures. But if you fall apart when faced with the inevitable changes that life brings, you will never move forward.

We often resist change, but really, who would want a life without it? Some of our greatest experiences, growth, and rewards come to us as the result of moving to a new place, switching jobs, following a different course of study, or moving into a better relationship.

Our lives are a progression from childhood through adolescence and adulthood into our senior years. To not change would be impossible and deadly dull. Sometimes we have to be patient. We can't always control or even influence change, and the changes that we want may not happen when we want them to.

There are two major types of change that tend to challenge us and disrupt our day-to-day lives. The first happens to us. The second happens within us. We can't control the first, but we can and should control the second.

I had no say in my parents' decision to move to the United States, any more than I did about being born without arms or legs. They were beyond my influence. But just as with my disability, I had the power to determine how I would deal with the move to the United States. I came to accept it and to dedicate myself to making the best of it.

You have that same ability to deal with unwanted or unexpected changes in your life. Often you can be blindsided by rapid and unexpected shifts in your circumstances—a loved one dies, a job is lost, an illness strikes, an accident occurs—so that you may not recognize at first that a major life-changing event is under way. Your first step in mastering an unwanted or sudden alteration is to be alert to them and quick to recognize that you are about to enter a new phase, for better or worse. Just being aware of that reduces the stress. Keep in mind thoughts like *Okay, this is all new. It will seem a bit strange. I will need to stay calm, not panic, and be patient. I know it will all work out for the best.*

When we moved to the United States, I had plenty of time to think about all the ways our lives were changing, yet at some moments I felt overwhelmed and disoriented. Sometimes I felt like screaming, "I just want to go back home to my real life!"

Sorry to say, mate, but you will probably have those moments too. I look back on mine now and see the humor in them, especially since now I love living in California. Hopefully you'll be able to laugh at yourself one day just as I did. You should understand that frustrations and anger are natural emotions when going through a major transition. Give yourself some slack and time to adjust. It helps to prepare yourself for unexpected jolts now and then. It's like moving to a new city: you have to give yourself time to find your way, get acclimated, and discover where you fit in.

EXPECT THE UNEXPECTED

Culture shock set in early and often during my first few weeks in America. In fact, on the very first day of school I had a bit of a panic when the entire class stood to recite the Pledge of Allegiance. We didn't do anything like that in Australia. I felt like I'd walked into a club that I didn't belong to.

Then one day all the alarms went off and the teachers told us to get under our desks! I thought aliens were attacking, but it was just a disaster drill for earthquakes. *Earthquakes!*

Of course I got the usual nervous glances, rude questions, and odd comments about my lack of limbs. I could not believe how curious American middle-school kids were about how I managed in the restroom. I prayed for an earthquake, just to stop the endless interrogations about my toilet tactics.

I had to adjust also to the constant shuffle from class to class. Back in Australia all my subjects were taught in one room. We didn't move around all day like kangaroos in the outback. At Lindero Canyon Middle School, it seemed like all we did was hop from one classroom to the next.

I was not handling this major life change very well. I'd always been a good student, but I quickly fell behind in my new school. They had no room in the regular sixth-grade classes so they'd put me in an advanced studies program, but my grades were retreating. Looking back, I can see that I was just stressed out. And why wouldn't I have been? My whole life had been packed up and transported across the globe.

We didn't even have our own house anymore. My father was working for Uncle Batta, and we were living with him and his family in their big house until we found our own. I didn't see much of my parents because they were busy finding work, commuting to work, or looking for a place to live.

I hated it. I was overwhelmed, mentally, emotionally, and physically. So I made like a turtle and withdrew into my shell. During recess and lunch hours, I went off on my own, sometimes hiding behind the bushes near the playground. My favorite hideout, though, was in one of the music rooms overseen by Mr. McKagan, the band and music teacher.

Mr. McKagan, who is still on the staff at Lindero Canyon, is a terrific teacher. He was so popular, he was like a rock star at the school, teaching (I think) eight or nine classes a day. His brother Duff is a legendary bass guitarist who has played with Guns N' Roses and other top rock bands. That was another strange aspect of moving from Australia to California. I felt like we'd left a perfectly normal family existence and landed in some surreal pop culture kingdom. We lived just outside Los Angeles and Hollywood, so we were always bumping into movie stars and television stars in the grocery store or at the mall. Half my classmates were aspiring or working actors. After school, I could turn on the television and watch a nice guy from my history class, Jonathan Taylor Thomas, ham it up on the popular television show *Home Improvement*.

My life had been altered in so many ways, I was simply overwhelmed. I'd lost all the confidence I'd worked so hard to build. My Australian classmates had accepted me, but in America I was a stranger in a strange land with a strange accent and an even stranger body. Or at least that's how I felt. Mr. McKagan saw that I was hiding out in his music rooms, and he tried to encourage me to go out and mix with the other students. But I just couldn't get motivated.

I was fighting a change I couldn't control instead of focusing on what I could adjust, my attitude and my actions. Really, I should have known better. I was only twelve years old, but I'd already learned to focus on my abilities instead of my disabilities. I'd accepted my lack of limbs and I'd managed to become a pretty happy and self-sufficient kid. But this move threw me for a loop.

Have you ever noticed that when you enter into one of those major transitional periods in your life, your senses seem heightened? When you go through a bad breakup, doesn't every movie and television show seem to have a hidden message aimed at you? Don't all the songs on the radio seem to be about your very own aching heart? Those heightened emotions and senses may be survival tools triggered when you are stressed or thrown into unfamiliar situations. They put you on high alert, and they can be valuable.

I still remember that as distressed as I was about leaving Australia, I always found peace and comfort gazing at the mountains or watching the sun set on the beach in my new environment. I still think California is a beautiful place, but it seemed even more beautiful then.

Whether positive or negative, change can be a powerful and scary experience, which is why your first reaction may be to fight it. When I took business classes in college, I learned that most major corporations have executives who are the designated "change agents." Their job is to rally reluctant employees behind big transitions, whether it's a merger, or a new division, or a new way of doing business.

As the president of my own business, I've learned that each employee has his or her own way of dealing with new initiatives or alterations in our mission. There will always be a few people who get excited about new experiences, but mostly people resist because they are comfortable with the status quo, or they fear their lives will change for the worse.

CHANGE RESISTANT

Everyone knows nothing stays the same forever, but strangely, when outside events or other people force us out of our comfort zones, we often become fearful and insecure. Sometimes we grow angry and resentful. Even when people are in a bad situation—a violent relationship, a dead-end job, or a dangerous environment—they often refuse to take a new path because they would rather deal with the known than the unknown.

I recently met George, a physical therapist and fitness coach. I told him that I was having a problem with my back and that I needed some exercises to strengthen it but I couldn't get motivated to work out because I was so busy traveling and running my company. George's response was classic: "Hey, if you want to deal with that pain getting worse and worse for the rest of your life, good luck to you."

He mocked me! I felt like giving George a head butt. But then I realized he was motivating me, forcing me to deal with the fact that if I was not willing to adjust my lifestyle, I would pay the consequences.

He was saying, *Nick, you don't have to change if you don't feel like it, but the only person who can help your back feel better is you.*

I was a good example of a bad example with my resistance to a lifestyle adjustment. But people in far worse circumstances resist moves that would greatly improve their lives. Often they are afraid to give up even terrible situations if it means shifting into an unfamiliar situation. And many people refuse to accept responsibility for their own lives. President Barack Obama stressed the importance of personal responsibility when he said, "We are the change we have been waiting for." But some people fight the tide, even when it threatens to drown them.

For some people, taking responsibility is a lot more daunting than taking a pass. When life deals you a card that ruins your hand and upsets your plans, you can blame the universe, your parents, and the kid who stole your sandwich in the third grade. But in the end, blaming does nothing for you. Taking responsibility is the only way to master the detours and shifting conditions along your life's path. My experiences have taught me that making a positive change has five necessary stages.

1. Recognizing the need to change

Sadly, we are often slow to recognize the need to make a move. We settle into a routine, even if it isn't all that comfortable, and we choose inaction over action simply out of laziness or fear. Often it takes something really scary to make us recognize that we need a new plan. My attempted suicide was one such moment for me. I had been hanging on for years, putting on a brave face most of the time, but inside I was haunted by dark thoughts that if I could not change my body, I'd end my life. When I reached the point where I nearly let myself drown, I recognized it was time to take responsibility for my own happiness.

2. Envisioning something new

A friend of mine, Ned, recently had the sad task of convincing his parents to move out of their home of forty years and into a senior living center, a nursing home. His father's health was failing, and the burden of caring for him had endangered his mother's life too. His parents did not want to move. They preferred to stay in their home, surrounded by neighbors they knew. "We are happy here. Why would we leave?" they said.

Ned talked it over with his parents for more than a year before he convinced them to visit a very nice senior citizens community just a few blocks from their home. They'd formed an image of "old folks' homes" as cold and dreary places where "old people go to die." Instead, they found a clean, warm, and lively place where many of their former neighbors were living and enjoying active days. It had a medical clinic staffed with doctors and nurses and therapists who could take over some of the care for Ned's father that had weighed so heavily on his mother.

Once his parents had a vision of the new place, they agreed to move there. "We never thought it could be so nice," they said.

If you have difficulty moving from where you are to where you need to go, it may help to get a clear vision of where the move will take you. This may mean scouting out a location, trying new relationships, or shadowing someone in a career you might want to pursue. Once you are more familiar with the new place, it will be easier to leave the old one.

3. Letting go of the old

This is a tough stage for many people. Imagine you are climbing a rock wall in the mountains. You are halfway up the wall, hundreds of feet above the valley floor. You have just come to a small ledge. It's scary, and you know you would be vulnerable if the wind picked up or a storm moved in, but on that ledge you have at least some sense of security.

The problem is that to keep moving up, or even to head back down, you have to abandon the security of that ledge and reach for another hold. Letting go of that sense of security, however tenuous, is the challenge, whether you are rock climbing or taking a new path in life. You have to release your hold on the old and grab on to the new. Many people freeze at this stage, or they start to make the move but then get scared and chicken out. If you find yourself in this situation, think of yourself as climbing a ladder. To move to the next rung, you must give up your grip and reach for the next one. Release, reach, and raise yourself up, one rung at a time!

4. Getting settled

This can be another tricky stage for people. They may have let go of the old and moved up to the new, but until they attain a certain comfort level, they can still be tempted to go running back. It's the *Okay, I'm here, now what?* stage.

The key to settling in is to be very careful about the thoughts that play out in your head. You have to screen out panic-mode thoughts like *Oh my gosh, what did I do?* and focus forward along the lines of *This is a great adventure!*

In my first few months in the United States as a boy, I struggled with the acceptance stage mightily. I spent many days and nights twitching uncomfortably in my bed, fretting about my new environment. I hid out from other students, fearing rejection and mockery. But slowly, gradually, I came to enjoy certain aspects of my new home. For one thing, I had cousins here too; I just hadn't known them as well as my cousins back in Australia. My American cousins turned out to be great people. Then there were the beach and the mountains and the desert, all within easy reach.

Then, just as I began to think maybe California USA wasn't so bad, my parents decided to return to Australia. When I got older and finished college, I moved right back to California. Now, it feels like home to me!

5. Keep growing

This is the best stage of making a successful transition. You've made the leap, and now it's time to grow in the new environment. The fact is that you really can't keep growing without change. Although the process can be stressful and even downright painful emotionally and even physically, the growth is usually worth it.

I've seen that in my business. A few years ago I had to restructure my company. That meant letting some people go. I am horrible at firing people. I absolutely hate it. I'm a nurturing kind of guy, not a bloke who likes to bring the bad news down on those I care about. I still have nightmares about firing staff members whom I'd come to know and love as friends. But looking back, my company never would have been able to grow if I hadn't made that change. We've reaped the rewards. I can't say that I'm glad to have let go those former employees; I miss them still.

Growing pains are a sign that you are stretching and reaching for new heights. You don't have to enjoy them, but know that they always come before a breakthrough that leads to better days.

CHANGING THE WORLD

In my travels I've observed people in each of these stages of change, especially during the 2008 trip to India that I described before. I went to speak in Mumbai, India's largest city and the second most populated city in the world. Once known as Bombay, Mumbai is on India's west coast, on the Arabian Sea, and serves as its financial and cultural center.

This city, home to both great wealth and terrible poverty, has been in the public spotlight because it served as the setting for the Academy Award–winning movie *Slumdog Millionaire*. As great as it is, that film offered only brief glimpses into the horrors of Mumbai's slums and the sexual slave trade that flourishes in a city dominated by Hindus and Muslims, with only a small population of Christians.

It's estimated that more than half a million people are forced to sell their bodies in Mumbai. Most are kidnapped from small villages in Nepal, Bangladesh, and other rural areas. Many of the women are *devadasi*, worshippers of a Hindu goddess who were forced into prostitution by their "priests." Some of the prostitutes are male *hijras*, castrated men. They are packed into filthy tenement houses and forced to have sex with at least four men a night. They have spread the AIDS virus rapidly, and millions have died.

At one point I was taken to the red-light district known as the "Street of Cages" in Mumbai to see the suffering there and to speak to the victims of slavery. I had been invited by the Reverend K. K. Devaraj, founder of Bombay Teen Challenge, which works to rescue people from sexual slavery and help them find better, healthy lives.

Uncle Dev, who also operates a home for AIDS orphans, feeding programs, medical centers, an HIV/AIDS clinic, and a rescue operation for drug-addicted "street boys," had seen my videos, so he hoped that I could serve as a change agent in Mumbai. He wanted me to convince women working as prostitutes to flee slavery and to move into his shelters. Reverend Devaraj says that each enslaved woman is a "precious soul and valuable pearl."

Bombay Teen Challenge is such a force for good in the slums of Mumbai that the pimps and madams allow Uncle Dev and his team, who are Christians, to come in and speak to them, even though most are Hindu. They welcome that calming influence even though the Bombay Teen Challenge team constantly tries to convince the prostitutes to accept Christ and to leave the brothels for better lives.

Bit by bit, this ministry works to change the hearts of these enslaved women. The average girl is kidnapped between the age of ten and thirteen. They are lured from small rural villages, and most are very naïve. If a girl is wary, the recruiters try to win over her parents, telling them she will earn fifty times the average wage. Or, sadly, they buy the girl from her parents, an all-too-common occurrence. The people who recruit and transport them are the first in a long line of cruel abusers. Once the girls are captive, the pimps take control, telling them, "You work for us now, whether you like it or not."

While in Mumbai, we interviewed several former sex slaves who'd been freed by Bombay Teen Challenge. Their stories, each one heartbreaking, are unfortunately not unusual. If they refused to be prostitutes, they were beaten, raped, and put in cages in dark and filthy underground compounds where they couldn't even stand up. There they were starved, abused, and brainwashed all the more until they became submissive. Then they were sent to the brothels where they were told that they had been purchased for seven hundred U.S. dollars and that they had three years to work off the debt as prostitutes. Former sex slaves told us they'd been required to have sex hundreds of times, with two dollars applied to their debt each time.

Most think they have no other options. The pimps tell them

that their families will never take them back because of the shame they've brought to them. Many contract sexually transmitted diseases or have children as the result of their prostitution and so they feel they have nowhere else to go.

As horrendous as life is for these girls and women, they often are afraid to make a change. Without faith, they lose hope, and then they lose their humanity. They despair of ever making it out of slavery and the slum. Psychologists often see the same resistance to escaping in women who are in abusive relationships. They may live in fear and pain, but they refuse to leave the abuser because they are more fearful of the unknown. They have lost their ability to dream of a better life, so they can't see it.

You may clearly see that these sex slaves should flee their terrible lives, but do you always see your own situation with such clarity? Have you ever felt trapped in circumstances, then discovered that the only trap was your own lack of vision, lack of courage, or failure to see that you had better options?

To make a change, you must be able to envision what lies on the other side. You have to have hope and faith in God and in your ability to find something better.

The Bombay Teen Challenge recognizes that women who have been enslaved have difficulty seeing a way out because they are so beaten down, isolated, and threatened. Some say they can't believe that they are worthy of love or even decent treatment.

I witnessed firsthand the suffering in the brothels and slums of Mumbai, and I also saw the miracles that Uncle Dev and his dedicated missionaries are performing among the sex slaves and their children, known as "sparrows," who often live homeless, on the streets.

They took me from one house to another. In the first I was introduced to an old woman who rose slowly from the floor as we entered. She was a madam who, through an interpreter, invited me in to "preach to my whores and inspire them to be better."

The madam introduced me to a woman who looked to be in her forties. She told me that she'd been kidnapped from her rural home at the age of ten and forced into prostitution.

"I worked off my debt and was free to go at thirteen," she said through an interpreter. "I went out into the street for the first time, and I was beaten and raped. Still I made my way back to my family, but they didn't want anything to do with me anymore. I came back here and returned to work as a prostitute. Then I had two children, and one died. Two days ago I found out that I have AIDS, so my pimp fired me. And now I have a child to look after and nowhere to go."

From our perspective, you and I may see that she had options, but in her much narrower circumstance there seemed to be no alternatives. Understand that sometimes you may not see a way out, but know that change is always possible. When you can't find an alternate path, look for help. Seek guidance from those with a wider perspective. Whether it's a friend, a family member, a professional counselor, or a public servant, don't ever fall into the trap of thinking there is no escape. There is always a way out!

This woman was just twenty years old. I prayed with her. We told her that she could leave the brothel and live in housing provided by Bombay Teen Challenge while also receiving medical treatment at their clinic. Once we opened her eyes and showed her the way out to a more caring world, she was not only willing to change, she found faith as well.

"Hearing you speak, I know God chose not to heal me of HIV/AIDS because I can bring other women to Christ," she said. "I have nothing left, but I know God is with me."

The peace and hope in her eyes took my breath away. She was so beautiful in her faith. She said she knew God had not forgotten her, that He had a purpose for her even as she faced death. She was a changed woman who had transformed her suffering into a force for good. Amid so much poverty, despair, and cruelty, she was a radiant example of the power of God's love and the strength of the human spirit.

Uncle Dev and his missionary team have developed a number of methods for convincing Mumbai's sex slaves to leave their dangerous situations. They provide child care and schools so that kids can learn about Jesus and His love for them. The kids then tell their mothers that they too are loved and that they can move to a better life. I encourage you to embrace change that elevates your life and to be a force for change that uplifts the lives of others too.

NINE

Trust Others, More or Less

When I was eleven years old, my parents took me to the beach on Australia's Gold Coast. My mum and dad walked down the coast a bit, and I was just chillin' in the sand near the edge of the water, watching the waves and basking in the breeze. I covered up with an oversize T-shirt so I wouldn't get sunburned.

A young woman came walking along the beach, and as she approached, she smiled and said, "That's quite impressive!"

"What do you mean?" I asked, knowing that she wasn't referring to my huge biceps.

"How long did it take you to bury your legs like that?" she said.

I realized that she thought I'd hidden my legs in the sand somehow. Feeling mischievous, I played along.

"Oh, I had to dig such a long time," I said.

She laughed and strolled by, but I knew she could not resist a second look so I waited. Sure enough, just as her head swiveled for a parting glance, I popped up and hopped toward the water.

She didn't say anything, though she stumbled a bit as she scurried down the beach.

Sometimes as a boy I resented such moments, but eventually I came to be more patient and understanding of others. Like that woman, I've learned that sometimes there is more to people than you first suspect, and sometimes there is less.

The art of reading people, relating to them, engaging with them, and stepping into their shoes, knowing whom to trust and how to be trustworthy is critical to your success and happiness. Few people succeed without the ability to build relationships based on mutual understanding and trust. We all need not just someone to love but also friends, mentors, role models, and supporters who buy into our dreams and help us achieve them.

To build your Dream Team of supporters who have your best interests at heart, you must first prove yourself trustworthy by standing up for them. Your mates will treat you the way you treat them. If you invest in their success, support them, encourage them, and give them your honest feedback, you can expect them to do the same for you. If they don't, you should move on and find someone who wants to be on your team.

We are social by nature, but if your relationships aren't what you'd like them to be, you may not be giving enough thought to how you interact with others and what you put in and take out of your relationships. One of the biggest mistakes you can make is to try and win friends only by telling them about yourself: your fears, frustrations, and pleasures. The truth is that you win friends by learning about them and finding shared interests to build bonds that provide mutual benefits.

Building a relationship is like building a savings account; you can't expect to take anything out of it if you haven't put something into it. We all need to tune up our relationship skills from time to time by evaluating our approach to them and looking at what is working and what is not.

HOW DO YOU RELATE TO OTHERS?

A strong sense of purpose, high hopes, abiding faith, self-love, a positive attitude, fearlessness, resilience, and mastery of change will take you a long way, but no one makes it alone. To be sure, I value my ability to take care of myself. I worked hard to become as independent as possible. But I am still dependent on the people around me, just as we all are to a great degree.

Often I am asked, "Isn't it hard to rely so much on others?" And my response is, "You tell me." Whether you acknowledge it or not, you depend on those around you nearly as much as I do. Some tasks I need help managing, but no one on this earth succeeds without benefiting from the wisdom, the kindness, or the helping hands of someone else.

We all need supportive relationships. We all must engage with kindred spirits. To do that effectively, we must build trust and prove ourselves trustworthy. We must understand that most people instinctively act out of self-interest, but if you show them that you are interested in them and invested in their success, most will do the same for you.

MAKING CONNECTIONS

When I was a boy, my mum often took me shopping or to other public places, and while she went about her business, I'd spend hours observing faces in the crowd from my wheelchair. I'd study them as they passed by and try to guess what they did for a living and what their personalities were like. Of course, I never knew whether my instant profiles were correct, but I did become a serious student of body language, facial expressions, and reading people in general.

This was mostly a subconscious process, but when I look back and reflect, I realize I was instinctively developing some very important skills. Since I lack the arms to defend myself, or the legs to run, it was important for me to quickly assess whether I could trust someone or not. It's not that I consciously worried about being attacked, but I was more vulnerable than most, and so I became more "people aware" than most.

I'm sensitive to the moods, emotions, and sounds of those around me. This may sound a little strange, but my antennae are so finely tuned that when someone puts a hand on my wheelchair armrest, it's almost like we are holding hands. I get this weird feeling that a physical connection has been made, just as if we were shaking or holding hands. Whenever my friends or family members put their hands on my chair, I feel this warmth and acceptance.

My lack of limbs has affected the way I relate to people as a professional speaker. I don't have to worry about one of the primary concerns of most speakers—what to do with my hands. I've worked on communicating with my facial expressions, and especially my eyes, rather than my hands. I can't make gestures to emphasize points or convey emotion. I worked at varying the width of my eyes and changing my facial expressions to convey emotions, and to hold the attention of my audiences.

My sister recently teased me: "Nick, you really do love eye contact. When you speak to someone, you look into their eyes with this intensity. That's the only way I can describe it."

Michelle knows me well. I look into the eyes of other people because they are windows to the soul. I love eye contact. I admire the beauty of people, and I find it, often, in their eyes. We can all find something bad or imperfect in others, but I choose to look at the gold within them.

"It's also your way of keeping the conversation real and sincere," my little sister said. "I can see it when you talk to my friends. You get straight to the core of the person, and you capture their attention so that they soak up every word you tell them."

I've learned to engage quickly by looking into the eyes of the people I meet and asking questions or making comments to find a common ground. Before back pains limited my huggability, one of my favorite ice breakers was to say, "Come and give me a hug."

By inviting people to come close and make contact, I hoped

to make them feel comfortable with me. Reaching out to others, bonding with them, finding a common ground are relationship skills that everyone should master. They determine how well we interact with those around us.

SKILL SETS

"People skills" is a widely used term but is rarely well defined. We all like to think we have great people skills, just like most of us are under the illusion that we are great drivers. My brother teases that I'm the world's worst backseat driver even though I've never had a legal driver's license. According to him, my people skills are a work in progress. Yours should be a work in progress too.

No one should take for granted skills that are critical to success and happiness. You can live a life without limits, but you can't live a life without trusting relationships. That is why you should always self-monitor, assess, and work to develop and refine the ways in which you engage with those around you. Psychologists say that our ability to build bonds of trust and mutually supportive relationships depends on a few primary people skills. These include the ability to:

- Read emotions and moods

- Listen attentively to what others say and how they say it

- Assess, comprehend, and react to nonverbal signals from others

- Navigate any social setting or gathering

- Bond quickly with others

- Turn on the charm in any situation

- Practice tact and self-control

- Demonstrate care for others with actions

Now let's look at each of those basic people skills in more detail.

Taking a Read

Reading body language, tone of voice, facial expressions, and the look in someone's eyes is a skill we all have to some degree. We really can't help but pick up these signals. Most people can even tell when someone is pretending to be angry but isn't, or is faking pain just for attention. Psychologists say this skill improves as we age, and women are generally better at it than men. I wasn't surprised to learn that women with children are especially good at it. My mum could read me like a book. She often seemed to know before I did when I felt sick, hurt, frustrated, or sad.

Listening to Understand

This is what your parents were talking about when they said "God gave you just one mouth but He gave you two ears, so you should listen twice as much as you speak." Too often we don't listen to understand. Instead, we listen just enough so we can respond. To really connect, you have to take into account the feeling behind the words, not just the words themselves. I'm no relationship expert, but I've seen my fellow men struggle with this. Women are known to be more intuitive and can become frustrated with men, who tend to be more literal. They tune in to the words rather than the emotions.

Get It and Go with It

It's one thing to listen and observe carefully, but it's even more important to take what you hear and observe, accurately assess it, and then act upon it. The people who do this well tend to have the best relationships and to be high achievers in their work. It can also be an important survival skill. *The New York Times* reported a story about two American soldiers on patrol in Iraq who saw a parked car with two young boys inside. The windows were rolled up even though it was 120 degrees outside. One of the soldiers asked the other, his patrol sergeant, if he could offer the boys some water and took steps toward the car.

The sergeant looked at the entire scene around them and sensed danger. He ordered the patrol to fall back. Just as his soldier turned around, a bomb exploded inside the car. The two boys were killed. The soldier who wanted to help them was hit by shrapnel but survived.

Later the sergeant would recall that when he saw his soldier move toward the car, "My body got cooler; you know that *danger* feeling." Other subtle clues had tweaked his antennae earlier. No shots had been fired at them that morning, which was unusual, and overall the streets had been quieter than they were on a typical day.

Studies of veteran soldiers have shown how they rely on their ability to quickly read and interpret their surroundings based on sensations, body language, or anomalies that "just don't fit." This is critical not just for relationships but for survival, for them and for us.

Work the Room

Knowing how to act appropriately and fit in—whether at a church social, a private country club, an employee picnic, or a simple dinner—is another important people skill. You have to respect where you are. When visiting foreign lands, I often ask my host or interpreter to help me understand local customs and traditions so that I don't make a mistake that alienates my audience.

There are certain actions you do while dining at home that you should never do during meals in certain countries. In most places belching is considered the height of rudeness, but in some places a good raucous burp is considered a compliment to the chef. On a more serious note, there are topics you should avoid in certain settings. Mentioning old conflicts, politics, and in some cases, even religion can only lead to trouble.

But you can always find common ground for engaging with others. As I've matured, I've learned that listening is the most valuable skill for engaging others, especially when you are "working the room" in a large crowd.

Bond Ability

We bond with others not just through words but through our expressions and body language, which includes how we position ourselves in relation to others. We often aren't aware of our positioning until someone who is spatially impaired invades our personal space. Close talkers, for example, may be trying to bond, but they tend to send people fleeing. It's a difficult line to judge, because we welcome some people into our personal space more than others. A friend once shot me a look of utter panic at a party because he'd been backed into a corner by four people vying for his attention. They towered over him, and he looked a bit like a fox cornered by the hounds.

Charisma Campaign

I don't have a problem capturing anyone's attention, but holding on to it is another challenge altogether. When I meet people, they are intrigued by my body but not always comfortable looking at it. I have just a few seconds to overcome that by turning on the charm. With kids and teens especially, I'll make jokes about "lending a hand" or something costing me "an arm and a leg," so they can see that I've heard all the comments and that I can laugh along with them. I think the real secret to charisma is making each person you meet feel that they have your complete attention when they speak to you.

Tactical Unit

We all tend to think we are tactful and thoughtful of other people, but I know I sometimes fall short. My brother loves to remind me that I bossed him around when we were younger. Aaron had to put up with a lot. Even when my parents were both home, he served as my caregiver because we were always together. He'll tell you that I could get a little crazy with my demands. One morning, for example, his friend Phil visited us. He walked into the kitchen at breakfast time, so I asked Aaron and Phil if they wanted some bacon and eggs.

"Sure, thanks, Nick!" Phil said.

I set about fixing him bacon and eggs. I did this by yelling, "Okay, Aaron, can you get me some eggs, and I also need you to fetch the pan. Oh, and put the pan on the stove. Crack the eggs in the pan, and I'll take over once they're cooked."

As Aaron got older and bigger, he found a way to deal with my bossy ways. Whenever he decided that I was being too demanding, he'd threaten to put me in a cabinet drawer, shut it, and leave me there. So I had to develop tactful people skills, or I would have been filed away forever!

Walk the Talk

We've all heard of those who "talk the talk but don't walk the walk." You can be a great listener, a highly empathetic, engaging, charming, and tactful person, but if you don't step up and reach out to other people when the situation requires it, then all your other skills are meaningless. Just saying "I feel for you" doesn't cover it. Your actions speak louder than your words.

In your work relationships, this means not only doing your job and striving to be successful but helping others do their jobs and supporting them in their efforts to succeed.

TUNING IN

To master these people skills, you must place your own self-interests, concerns, and agendas on hold and dial in to those around you. It's not about being the center of attention or the funniest person in the room; it's about engaging with other people on their terms and making them comfortable enough to invite you into their lives.

The depth of our relationships varies from those we engage with briefly (store clerks, waitresses, the mailman, the guy next to you on the plane) to those we interact with regularly (neighbors, co-workers, customers, and clients), and finally to people who are a big part of our lives (our best friends, spouses, and family members). Each level requires people skills of some sort, the ability to relate to and interact in harmony with others.

Helping Hands

There is one more people skill that is often disdained or overlooked, but one I'm quite familiar with: the willingness and the humility to ask for help when you need it. Jesus, the son of God, rarely walked alone on this earth. He was usually in the company of one or more of his disciples. You should never feel that you have to go it alone. Asking for help is not a sign of weakness. It is a sign of strength. The Bible says, "Ask and it will be given to you; seek and you will find; knock and the door will be opened to you. For everyone who asks receives; he who seeks finds; and to him who knocks, the door shall be opened."

A few years ago my heavy travel schedule led me to decide to return to using caregivers, which is something I tried to avoid for a long time. When I was younger, I wanted to prove that I could survive day by day without depending on other people. Being independent was important to me. I needed to know, for my own peace of mind and my self-esteem, that I could live on my own if necessary.

But as my public speaking career took off and invitations to speak came from all over the globe, I realized that I was burning up too much energy taking care of myself, especially on the road. To speak to as many people in as many different places as I do, you have to be fully engaged and full of energy. I went back to employing caregivers even though someday, down the road, I hope to have a wife and family and again be independent.

When you have a caregiver, lacking people skills is not an option. Even if their pay is good, you can't expect someone to feed you, travel with you, shave you, dress you, and sometimes carry you around if they don't like you. Luckily, I've always had good relationships with mine—though they've sometimes been put to the test. I did not have a full-time caregiver until 2005, when Craig Blackburn, who'd been inspired by my speaking and testimony in church, contacted me. He offered to work as my caregiver, driver, and coordinator for a three-week speaking tour along the sunny Queensland coast. I was a little nervous about doing the tour with someone I didn't know well, but I prayed on it, checked his credentials, and decided I could trust him. Craig proved to be very helpful, allowing me to save my energies for my speaking and other duties.

In my determined effort to prove my independence while also building a career that required intense travel, I'd been too proud to ask for help, even when it made sense to do so. You shouldn't make the same mistake. Know your limitations. Protect your health and sanity by doing what is only human: reaching out when conditions call for it. But remember, to ask something of friends or co-workers is rude unless you've shown interest and consideration for them. No one owes you anything more than you have given to them.

A few of my caregivers have been friends, family members, and volunteers over the years, but most are paid to assist me because the job is demanding, given my hectic schedule. I began using caregivers more and more while traveling in the United States in 2006. A fellow named George had volunteered to serve as my driver and caregiver on that tour, but he showed up driving a wreck of a little car that was loud and stinky and, to my astonishment, had a gaping hole in the floor! It was a bit of a shock. I had visions of falling through and being flattened by a trailing truck. I never felt entirely safe in that car, but George proved to be a loyal supporter and a great caregiver.

One of my current caregivers, Bryan, was put to the ultimate test during my European speaking tour in the summer of 2008. We'd been traveling nonstop for about a week when we arrived for a one-night stay at a hotel in Timisoara, Romania, a beautiful city known as "Little Vienna," in the Transylvanian Alps. I'd always heard that this was a spooky corner of the planet, and my suspicions were confirmed.

Dead tired from lack of sleep, I was too weary to fret. This was the first night on the long tour where I was scheduled to catch some serious rest. Since I'd been having trouble sleeping, Bryan offered me a melatonin capsule, which is supposed to help your body deal with jet lag.

At first, I told him I'd better not take it. Because of my low body weight, I sometimes have strange reactions to supplements. Bryan convinced me it was safe, and just to be cautious, I took only a half-dose. Luckily I didn't swallow the entire capsule. I fell into a deep sleep right away.

On some tours I become overtired, and despite the tremendous effort it takes for me to sit up in bed, I'll do just that in my sleep, and then I'll begin speaking as if I'm addressing an audience. On this night I woke up Bryan in the next room because I was preaching! In Serbian!

Bryan woke me up before I roused all of Romania with my sleep-sermonizing, and we both realized then that we were sweating like crazy. We'd been cooking in the summer heat because while we slept, the room air conditioner had shut down. Naturally, we opened the windows to allow some fresh air to flow into our rooms. Then, bone-tired, we returned to our beds.

An hour later we again were awakened; this time we were being eaten alive by huge Transylvanian mosquitoes. (At least we hoped they were mosquitoes!) At that point I was dead tired, overheated, itching all over my body, and—a special bonus—lacking the usual scratching tools. It was torture!

At Bryan's suggestion, I took a shower to relieve the itching. Then he sprayed my swollen bug bites with an anti-itching first aid remedy. I returned to my bed, but ten minutes later I was hollering for Bryan again. My poor body was on fire! I'd had an allergic reaction to the anti-itching spray.

He scrambled to haul me into the shower again, and in the process he slipped, fell, and banged his head on the toilet, nearly knocking himself out! Exhausted, we just wanted to sleep, but our night of horrors was not yet over. With the air conditioner out, the room was just too hot. By this time I wasn't thinking like a sane person, so I told Bryan to lend me a pillow.

"The air conditioner is working in the hallway, so I'm sleeping out there," I told my baffled caregiver.

Bryan didn't have the strength to argue with me. He collapsed on his bed, and I crashed just outside the room, leaving the door open so he could hear me if I needed help. We snoozed like that for an hour or two before a total stranger stepped over me, marched into the room, and berated poor Bryan in broken English.

He ranted on for several minutes before we figured out that our intruder was furious because he thought Bryan had thrown me out in the hallway to sleep on the floor! We had a tough time convincing this would-be Good Samaritan that I was sleeping in the corridor by choice.

Once the stranger left, I crawled back into my bed. Bryan returned to his. But just as we finally drifted off to sleep, Bryan's cell phone rang. When he answered, a verbal blast pounded his ear. It was the coordinator of our speaking tour. Evidently our well-meaning intruder had not been convinced. He'd reported to hotel security that I'd been left in the hallway all night, and they'd raised heck with our coordinator, who was threatening to have poor Bryan tarred and feathered.

Now you can see why I normally employ three caregivers who rotate on shifts seven days a week. Bryan and I can laugh about our nightmarish night in Transylvania now, but it took several nights of sleeping in cool rooms, without bugs, to get over it.

One of the lessons I had to learn early in life was that it's okay to ask for help. Whether you've got all the standard body parts or not, there will be times when you simply can't go it alone. Yes, humility is a people skill and a God-given gift.

You have to be humble to ask others for help, whether it's a caregiver, a mentor, a role model, or a family member. When someone is humble enough to reach out for assistance, most people respond by giving of themselves and their time. If you act as though you have all the answers and don't need anyone else, you are less likely to attract support.

PANTLESS AND SPEECHLESS

As a child I was taught that all honor goes to God, and as a man I've come to realize that whatever good I accomplish is done not by me but through me. It seems God believes I need a lesson in humility now and then so that I never lose my ability to engage and bond with others. Sometimes those lessons are hard. Sometimes they are hilarious.

I was still living in Australia in 2002 when my cousin Nathan Poljak accompanied me to the United States to speak at a church camp. We arrived the night before the engagement and were seriously jet-lagged by the long flight. We overslept.

I was scheduled to rise early to teach a Bible class, but no one had the heart to wake me. I rose from my coma just about fifteen minutes before the class was to start. We were staying nearby, so I thought we could still make it. We rushed to the camp, but when we arrived, I realized I had to use the restroom. Now, believe it or not, that's something I can usually do on my own. I will never give away my secret techniques, but replacing zippers with Velcro proved to be a big help. Nathan offered to assist me because we were in such a hurry. He carried me into a public restroom stall and set me up to do my business.

Once I'd finished, Nathan came in to help me close up shop, and as we were completing the process, he dropped my shorts into the toilet bowl! We froze in horror with our mouths gaping as my dignity disappeared in a slow-motion whirlpool. There I stood, pantless and overdue for my Bible school lecture. I stared in horror at my cousin. He mirrored my shock. And then we both set to laughing like two loons of the loo. We couldn't even fish my pants out because we were yucking it up so wildly, and our ineptitude made us even sillier with glee. Nathan has the most infectious laugh, and when he starts in, I can't help myself. I'm sure people standing outside the restroom wondered what was so hilarious in stall number three.

My cousins and brother and sister helped me learn to laugh when I find myself in ridiculous situations, and this was certainly one of them. They've also taught me to lean on those willing to help and to ask for assistance when I'm feeling overwhelmed. I encourage you to do the same.

THE HAND-OFF

My caregivers have been terrific over the years, and I'm fortunate to have them stay in my life as friends after they've moved on to new work. Nearly all actually start out as friends or people I've met while speaking, then come to work with me. There is always a break-in period, of sorts, and often it's quite amusing.

People who've been with me awhile often say they quickly forget about my missing parts and my disability becomes irrelevant. That's great, all well and good, except when the person happens to be my caregiver. I can't tell you how many times I've asked a rookie caregiver to give me a drink of water and he'll try to hand me a glass. There is always this moment of pause with his hand extended, holding the glass in the air and waiting for me to take it. Then there follows a sudden rush of blood from the face of the caregiver as he realizes, *Oh my God! I just tried to hand a glass of water to a guy with no arms! What was I thinking!*

"It's okay," I tell them. "I'm used to it."

Chances are you don't need a trained person to be there for you twenty-four hours a day, seven days a week. But we all need caregivers of some sort, someone to share ideas with, someone who will always give us honest advice, or someone who serves as an encourager, mentor, or role model.

It takes humility and courage to admit that you don't know everything or that you could use a hand. I mentioned earlier that when you have a sense of purpose and have committed to pursuing your dreams, you will always have a few detractors. Fortunately others will also appear—sometimes where you least expect it—to give you a boost, or to offer guidance. You should be ready for them because bonding with them can change your life.

There are three types of guides whose relationships have impacted my life: Mentors, Role Models, and Fellow Travelers.

Mentors are people who've been where you want to go, but they are also supporters and encouragers who share your dreams and truly want you to succeed. Your parents are natural mentors, but if you are lucky you will find others willing to step up in that role throughout your life. One of my earliest was my mother's brother, my uncle Sam Radojevic, who still lives in Australia with his great wife and wonderful children. He has the heart of an entrepreneur, the ingenuity of an inventor, and the vision of an explorer. Uncle Sam is always open to new experiences, and when I was young he encouraged me to take wing. He told me that the only true obstacles in life are those we make for ourselves. His guidance and support gave me the courage to expand my vision.

I've known many people who carry the burden of regret throughout their lives, but Uncle Sam has never been one to look back. Even when he makes mistakes, he always pushes forward to the next opportunity with the irrepressible spirit of a child in love with life.

He loves to design and build motorcycles and bicycles, but he doesn't just do it for himself. He helped the government of Victoria start a program in which prisoners repair and restore old bicycles for disadvantaged children and adults who couldn't otherwise afford a bicycle. Thousands of bikes have gone out to the needy because of that program.

Uncle Sam encourages me to likewise keep looking ahead, and he has always believed in me even when I didn't believe in myself. I was thirteen when he told me, "Nicholas, you will shake the hands of presidents, kings, and queens someday." He believed even then that God had a big plan for me. What a great person to have as a mentor!

I encourage you to reach out for your own mentors. But understand that true mentors aren't just cheerleaders—they will tell you when they think you are wandering off course. You have to be willing to listen to their criticisms as well as their praise, knowing that they have your best interests at heart.

I also looked up to my cousin Duncan Jurisic. When I was a child, I'd often be afraid to inconvenience someone to take me to the loo, so he helped me come up with a line to remember. He said, "When you need to go, just let someone know." Not only did he and my other Vujicic cousins continue to love and support me, but Duncan and his mother, Danilka, helped me overcome my fears in the early days of my speaking career. Their family, who ran the Australian Hospitality Group in Melbourne, offered me their wise and valuable guidance.

Role Models have been where you want to go, but they aren't usually as close to you as mentors. Usually you watch them from afar, study their moves, read their books, and follow their careers as models for your own. Often these are celebrated figures in your field, people whose success has made them famous and respected. One of my long-term role models whom I've always wanted to meet is the Reverend Billy Graham. He has lived the words from Mark 16:15 that also are my inspiration: "Go into all the world and preach the Gospel to every creature."

There has to be a place somewhere between mentors and role

models for folks like Vic and Elsie Schlatter, whom I've visited at least once a year nearly every year of my life. They always inspire me to be a better Christian and a better person. They live in Australia, but they have planted more than sixty-five churches and missions in far-flung corners of the South Pacific. They are my models for making a difference as missionaries. They work quietly, without a lot of publicity, and they never puff themselves up, but they've made a world of difference for many, many souls.

As a teen Elsie had a vision of Jesus standing before her instructing her to "go." Elsie took that to mean that God wanted her to do missionary work one day. Vic worked for General Electric at a nuclear plant after they got married, but he and Elsie also started a church and began planning their first mission—to Papua New Guinea, a small tribal nation in the South Pacific that had very little exposure to Christianity. Small though the nation was, its three million people were dauntingly diverse, speaking more than seven hundred dialects.

Vic and Elsie fell in love with that part of the world, and they now live on the north coast of Australia. From that base they conduct mission work around the South Pacific. In addition to writing several books of his own on religion, Vic has translated the Scriptures into pidgeon English and other dialects for the indigenous tribes he and Elsie serve.

Identifying a **Fellow Traveler** is a bit tough for me because my life has followed a rather unconventional path. Fellow travelers are usually peers, co-workers, and others with similar goals to yours, who are walking on a parallel road. They might even be rivals, but friendly rivals. You encourage and support each other by practicing an abundance mentality rather than a scarcity mentality.

When you believe in abundance, you believe there are enough of God's blessings—enough fulfillment, enough opportunity, enough happiness, and enough love—out there for everyone. I encourage you to take that point of view because it opens you up to other

people. If you tend to think of the world as a place of scarce resources and limited opportunities, then you'll see fellow travelers as threats who'll take what is out there and leave nothing for
you. Competition can be healthy because it motivates you, and
you will always find others who want what you want. With an
abundance mentality, you believe there are rewards enough for everyone, so competition is more about striving to do your best and
encouraging others to do the same.

An abundance mentality allows you to walk alongside your
fellow travelers with feelings of camaraderie and mutual support.
I learned that in my friendship with Joni Eareckson Tada, who has
traveled a similar path to mine. As I described earlier, Joni was a
role model for me long before I knew her; she became a mentor,
helping me get established in the United States; and now she is a
fellow traveler, offering wise counsel and a sympathetic ear.

Another person who has been there for me in all sorts of ways is
Jackie Davison, who lived around the corner from my family when
I was a teenager. She was married with young children, but Jackie
always found time to listen to me as I spilled my guts about whatever was on my mind, good or bad. She was close enough in age that
she was more of a wise friend than a judgmental adult. I have such
love for her family, and I became an unofficial big brother to her
kids, helping them with their homework or just hanging out.

Back in 2002 I was having a rough time in my university studies and in my personal life, and it was distracting and disorienting.
I'd broken up with a longtime girlfriend and was very emotional.
So I went to Jackie and asked her to help me understand what had
happened. I poured out my heart, but she sat there with her hands
clasped, patiently listening without responding. Suddenly it hit me
that as I was unloading all this emotional baggage on her, she wasn't
reacting. Finally I stopped and said, "What should I do? Tell me!"
She smiled and her eyes sparkled as she said simply, "Praise God."

Confused and frustrated, I said, "Praise God for what?"

"Just praise God, Nick."

I stared at the floor thinking, *That's all she has to say? This woman is something else!*

Then it hit me that Jackie was telling me to trust in God and that He hadn't forgotten me. She was telling me that I should put faith not in the wisdom of man but in the power of God. She was telling me to surrender to God and to thank Him, even though I didn't feel He deserved thanks. She was telling me to thank God in advance for blessings that would come of this pain. She has a powerful faith, and she always reminds me, when I feel confused or hurt, to surrender to God, because He has a plan for us all.

LIFE GUIDES

These "life guide" relationships are not always easy going. Your "guides" will give you a reality check or even a kick in the pants. But they care enough to make you really think about what you are doing, where you are going, why you are in the game, and what comes next. You want people like that in your life.

When I decided to become a public speaker and to encourage others to have faith, I shared the decision with my closest friends and family. Some were concerned, including my parents. The Apostolic Christian Church that I belong to has dispatched many missionaries over the years. They've built orphanages and helped many in need. When I told my parents that I wanted to speak about my faith to other denominations in churches around the world, they had misgivings about my health and concerns about whether this mission was truly what God wanted for me.

I listened to them because I knew they wanted me to be successful. You should do the same when your own Dream Team offers opinions about your plans, especially if you want them to remain invested in your success. Honor them and give careful thought to their advice and guidance. You don't have to accept it, but respect that they care enough to tell you even what you may not want to hear.

I respected my parents' concerns, but I felt God was calling me to be an evangelist. My mission then was to be obedient and patient and pray that they'd come to feel the same way. By God's grace, not only my parents but also the church accepted my calling. Its leaders stood behind me and ordained me as the church's first Minister of Evangelism.

There are no promises or guarantees that everyone you meet will want to help you. Some may even try to discourage you. They may have the best intentions and good reason to be worried. None of my parents' fears were irrational, but I prayed that their faith would overcome all those concerns.

Parents and their grown children often must agree to disagree and move on. The same holds true with other members of your Dream Team. You may be proven wrong when you go your own way. You may be proven right. In the end, being right isn't what's important.

I am so thankful that my parents and I can respect each other's opinions and decisions. By God's grace, our relationship withstood a test, and we emerged even closer than before because of our deep love and mutual respect. If we had not talked openly about our feelings, the outcome might not have been such a happy one.

I attended my church regularly as my base and did my best to mentor the young people there. But I also began to branch out, speaking to other churches, reaching out to people in a much wider area. I'm pleased to report that many of the young people have moved forward in their relationships with God, and I thank Him for that.

My mum and dad prayed for me and with me on the day in 2008 when I was officially ordained an evangelist, and that experience brought us to a new level of mutual love and respect. My parents knew that I was committed and dedicated to spreading the word of God. To have them all pray for me in front of the entire church congregation was something I'll never forget. I have to say that my parents are my strongest supporters, and they were right far more than they were wrong about the important decisions in my life.

You should never take relationships for granted, especially those with your closest family members. The rewards last a lifetime.

Take time now to evaluate your people skills, the quality of your relationships, and what you put into them. Are you trustworthy? Do you trust those closest to you? Are you attracting people willing to invest in your success? Are you honoring them? Are you putting into the relationship as much as you are taking out?

Each time I'm laughing and enjoying my family, I realize how much I live for such moments. My hope is to somehow convince them that San Diego beaches are better than Australian beaches so that I can always have them near. Hold your loved ones as close as you can, as long as you can.

The quality of your relationships has a huge impact on the quality of your life, so please treat them as precious. Don't take them for granted. The Bible says, "Two are better than one, because they have a good return for their work: If one falls down, his friend can help him up. But pity the man who falls and has no one to help him up!"

TEN

An Equal Opportunity Hugger

Joshua and Rebekah Weigel are award-winning filmmakers in Los Angeles dedicated to making movies that inspire as well as entertain. I'd never met them, but after they saw one of my videos, they were inspired to write a fictional screenplay with me in mind as the main character. As they were writing this script, the Weigels were trying to contact me through various channels, but since I was gadding about on a speaking tour, they couldn't reach me. Then one Sunday while they were attending church in Westlake Village, they ran into an old friend of theirs named Kyle.

"What are you doing now?" they asked Kyle.

"I'm working as a caregiver for this guy named Nick Vujicic," he said.

Not surprisingly, Joshua and Rebekah were stunned.

How amazing is that? How often does it happen that two dedicated filmmakers write a script for someone they've never met, then seek him out and offer to make a movie with him? It's fantastic, right? A dream come true!

Have you ever missed out on a wonderful chance because you didn't have your act together? Have you watched in despair as someone else ran through a door that you failed to see was open? Learn from those experiences, and buck up, mate! Walter Chrysler, founder of the Chrysler automotive company, once said that the reason so many people never get anywhere in life is that when opportunity knocks, they are out in the backyard looking for four-leaf

clovers. Today I see people buying lottery tickets instead of invest-
ing in their futures. Invest in your future by preparing with hard
work, dedicate yourself to your goals, and then watch for the right
time to make the leap.

If you feel you never get a shot, maybe it's because you aren't
locked, loaded, and ready to fire. You are responsible for your own
success. Take on that responsibility by preparing yourself to do
your best. When you get to the right place, the breaks will come.
If you have a chip on your shoulder, or you're hosting a pity party,
don't expect an invitation to the dance. Believe in yourself (have I
mentioned this already?). Believe in the possibilities for your life.
Believe in your value on this planet. If you don't feel worthy of
wings, you'll never get off the ground.

Break a sweat. Get your hands dirty. Hit the books. Thomas
Edison said opportunities are often missed because they are dressed
in overalls and look like work. Are you ready to do whatever it
takes?

I have to confess that when the Weigels first contacted me, I
wasn't paying attention. Poor Kyle was so excited for me. He tried
to tell me about his friends the filmmakers and the project they had
for me. "I have some friends who have a movie idea for you—" was
all he had a chance to say before I cut him off.

"Kyle, I'm too busy to talk to your friends right now," I said
crankily.

I'd been traveling a great deal and was edgy and tired. Oddly
enough, I'd recently been burned by another movie proposition.
After hearing just a basic outline of it (a feature-length film!), I'd
been excited about it for months. Then they sent me the script. It
turned out, the producers wanted me to portray a foul-mouthed,
tobacco-chewing character who spends most of the movie getting
lugged around in a potato sack slung over someone's back.

That was not the sort of role I wanted to begin my movie career, or end it. So I said no. Not every chance is worth taking. You have to be true to your values, incorporating them into your long-term goals. What mark do you wish to make? How do you want to be remembered? I didn't want my grandchildren to one day discover a DVD of a movie in which Grandpa Nick curses, drools tobacco juice down his chin, and lives like a degenerate. So I said thanks but no thanks to that first movie offer.

I loved the idea of making a movie, but I wasn't willing to abandon my values to do it. You may have to make a similar decision. Stay strong. Stick with your principles, but don't make the mistake I made: when I closed that first door, I also closed my mind.

That's why I shot down good old Kyle without a second thought when he cheerfully brought the Weigels' film project to me. I didn't see the future because I was looking in the rearview mirror. Big mistake.

Fortunately, the Weigels were not easily discouraged. They asked another friend to contact my media director. He read their screenplay, loved it, and brought it to me. Upon reading it, I realized Kyle deserved an apology. The Weigels' screenplay was about hope and redemption, subjects close to my heart.

And who better to star in a film short than me? Especially since the character they'd created for me was "Will the Limbless Man." As the movie begins, he is a snarly and depressed "freak" in a ragtag circus sideshow. Then, thanks to the kindness of others, Will is invited to join a far more benevolent circus troupe, where he becomes the star of a thrilling high-dive act.

I realized I'd better get off my "buts" and kick into action. I thanked Kyle and asked him to set up a meeting with the Weigels. Great events quickly unfolded. We met. We bonded. And I signed on the dotted line. My enthusiasm grew when I learned that a number of much more experienced actors already had agreed to take roles in the film.

This was a low-budget, fast-moving project, so I only had to clear a week's time on my schedule to complete my scenes. You will have to check the reviews to decide whether I have a future in show business, but *The Butterfly Circus* won the $100,000 grand prize at the Doorpost Film Project, which supports filmmakers who make hopeful films. Our little movie (which you can find at http://www.thedoorpost.com) was chosen over one hundred other short films featuring similar themes. The Doorpost grand prize brought it a lot of attention, and the Weigels are considering turning it into a full-length feature.

I just may dive into that project too. After all, not many actors can play the role of a limbless man who dives, swims, and pulls off the perfect Australian accent!

LIGHTS, CAMERA, ACTION!

To pursue your dreams you have to take action. Move it or lose it. Act or be acted upon. If you don't have what you want, consider creating what you want. God will light the path. Your chance of a lifetime, the door to your dreams is open. Your path to a purpose may present itself at any moment. Be ready for it. Do all you need to do. Learn all you need to know. If no one comes knocking, beat down a few doors. One day you'll step into the life you desire.

Be willing to put yourself out there, to embrace the moment. Earlier in my career, before I got back pain, I offered after each speech to give a hug to everyone who wanted one. To my amazement and gratitude, many lined up to share a word and a little squeeze. I was amazed because every person I met in those sessions had something unique to offer, a gift that I could take away. You need to feel the same way about opportunities. Even those that may not seem golden at first may shine once you've stepped up.

MAKE A BREAK

Even after you've built a powerful purpose and have developed huge reservoirs of hope, faith, self-esteem, positive attitudes, courage, resilience, adaptability, and good relationships, you can't just sit around and wait for a break. You have to seize upon every thread and weave a rope you can climb. Sometimes you'll even find that the boulder that fell and blocked your path left an opening that takes you to a higher place. But you have to have the courage and the determination to make the ascent.

One of our mottos at Life Without Limbs is "Another day, another opportunity." We don't simply have our slogan framed on a wall—we try to live it every day. Dr. Cara Barker, a psychologist and leadership coach, picked up on this when she wrote in a *Huffington Post* blog: "Nick Vujicic demonstrates that it's possible to awaken the heart, giving inspiration to others through a situation that nearly everyone on this Earth would find debilitating. A hero, Vujicic finds opportunity where most would find a dead end."

I'm humbled by her words. Growing up, it was often difficult for me to ever imagine myself being called a hero or an inspiration to anyone. I realized as a child that being angry about what I didn't have or frustrated about what I couldn't do only pushed people away from me, but when I looked for opportunities to serve others, they were drawn to me. I've learned not to wait around but to push ahead and make my own breaks because one always seems to lead to another. Every time I give a speech, attend an event, or visit a new part of the world, I meet people, learn about new organizations, and gather information that opens new opportunities down the road.

BLESSINGS IN DISGUISE

Dr. Barker correctly notes that once I switched my focus from my physical challenges to the blessings they presented, my life changed dramatically for the better. You can do the same. If I can recognize that the body God gave me is in many ways a great and wondrous gift, can you acknowledge that your own blessings may also be in disguise, perhaps even dwelling within an aspect of yourself that you see as your greatest weakness?

It's all about perspective. There is no hiding from life. You will take some hits. Unless you are blasted so hard you go into a coma, you will become frustrated, angry, and sad: *Been there, done that.* Still, I urge you to reject despair and bitterness. You can be buried by a giant wave, or you can ride it into shore. In the same way, challenging events in your life can push you down or lift you up. If you can breathe, be grateful. Use that gratitude to rise above depression and bitterness. Take one step, then another, build momentum, and create a life you love.

My physical handicap forced me to be bold and to speak to adults and other kids and to interact. And because of it I focused on my strengths in mathematics, so I always had a fallback profession if my speaking didn't work out. I've often thought that even some of the heartbreak I've endured because of my disability has benefited me by making me more compassionate toward others. In the same way, the failures I've experienced have made me much more appreciative of my successes and much more sympathetic to others who struggle and fail.

TAKING MEASURE

Not all opportunities are equal. At the beginning of this chapter, I wrote about embracing my first movie role, after turning down that earlier offer.

Now if you watch *The Butterfly Circus*, you will see that Will, my character, at the beginning of the movie isn't exactly an inspiring bloke. In fact, he's a bit repulsive because of the bitterness and despair he harbors in his heart. But I accepted this role because Will undergoes a transformation and overcomes his misery and resentment. Like a prickly caterpillar who transforms into a soaring butterfly, Will slowly sheds his suspicions and distrust and becomes a redeemed, loving, and inspiring person.

That's how I want to be known on this planet. How do you want to be known? In earlier chapters, we looked at the importance of having a purpose. When offers and breaks come your way, or when you create them for yourself, you must always ask yourself, *Does this match up with my purpose and my values?*

What qualifies as a good opportunity? Anything that takes you another step closer to your dream. There are other types, of course. Perhaps your friends invited you to go out and get wasted last night. Or maybe you played video games instead of preparing for a meeting at work or reading a book to sharpen your skills. The choices you make determine the quality of the life you lead.

Be thoughtful. Develop high standards and strict criteria for evaluating how you invest your time and energy. Base your choices not on what feels good in the moment but on what best serves your ultimate goals. Measure them according to your values and principles. I use the Grandpa Nick rule: *Will my grandkids be proud of this decision, or will they think their grandpappy was senile before his time?*

If you need to create a disciplined, formal process for assessing opportunities, sit down at your computer or with a pen and paper and create an Assessment Worksheet. For every opportunity that comes your way, write down the pros and cons and evaluate how each measures up to the values, principles, and goals you've chosen for your life. Then try to envision what will happen if you walk through the door, and what will happen if you close it instead.

If you still have trouble making a decision, take your worksheet to a trusted mentor, or a friend who believes in you and wants you to succeed. Talk through the pros and cons with them, and listen to their evaluation. Be open-minded, but also know that the responsibility is all yours. It's your life. You will reap the rewards or pay the price for your own decisions, so choose wisely.

ARE YOU READY?

Timing is another consideration when making these assessments. Sometimes, especially when you are young, tempting offers present themselves, but the timing may be off. You don't want to accept a job that you aren't qualified for or prepared to master, just as you shouldn't rush off on a luxury vacation you can't afford. The cost is too high. It will take you too long to recover.

One of the biggest mistakes I made early in my public speaking career was accepting an invitation to address a large audience before I'd really prepared for such a thing. It wasn't that I had nothing to say, I just hadn't organized my material or honed my presentation. As a result, I lacked the self-confidence to pull it off.

I stuttered and stammered through that speech. People were kind to me, but I had blown it. But I learned from the experience, recovered, and realized that I should seize only those moments that I am fully prepared to handle. That's not to say that you shouldn't jump on an offer or an option that forces you to stretch and grow. Sometimes we're more prepared than we realize, so God gives us a nudge that allows us to rise to the occasion and take a giant step toward our dreams. *American Idol*, the hit television show, is built on that concept. In each episode, many of the young contestants crack under the pressure, or realize that they simply aren't ready for stardom. But now and then a raw talent emerges and blossoms under the intense pressure. A select few, notably Carrie Underwood, Jennifer Hudson, Chris Daughtry, and Kelly Clarkson, have launched wonderful careers because they stretched, grew, and kept rising.

You need to weigh your options and carefully consider which stepping-stones will lead you to your goals, and which might cause you to slip and fall. Like me and the first movie role I was offered, you will come across opportunities that would serve a short-term goal but don't match up to your long-term objectives. Your decisions today will follow you into tomorrow. Often young people jump into relationships without considering whether the person is good for them over the long term. We're often reminded how security conscious we need to be when it comes to the Internet, whether it is our financial selves, our public reputation, or our private life that we need to protect. We're reminded that you've got to assume that everything you do—every photograph and video you appear in, every e-mail you send, every blog you write, every comment on your Web page—will show up in a search engine somewhere at some point and will exist on earth probably longer than you do. Just as you have to think carefully about how the things you post online without thinking can come back to haunt you, remember that the same is true in our lives when we evaluate opportunities that come our way. They have long-term consequences—which can help you or hurt you. The short-term benefits may look great, but what will the long-term repercussions be?

Step back and look at the big picture. Remember, you are often tested, but life itself is not a test. It's the real deal. The decisions you make every day impact the quality of your entire life. Assess carefully, then check your gut and your heart. If your gut tells you something's a bad idea, go with your gut. But if your heart tells you to leap at an opportunity—and it is aligned with your values and long-term goals—make the leap! There are still times when an offer arises that gives me goose bumps and I'm so excited that I want to just dive right in. But then I need to take a breath and pray for the wisdom to make the right decision.

THE RIGHT PLACE

If you have prepared yourself to the best of your ability but no doors have opened for you, then maybe you need to reposition yourself and your talents. If your dream is to be a world champion surfer, chances are Alaska won't offer many big waves, right? Sometimes you need to make a move to catch a break. I realized several years ago that if I wanted to develop a worldwide audience for my speaking career, I needed to move out of Australia and to the United States. I love Australia. Most of my family is still there. But Down Under was too remote a launching pad and didn't offer the options and the exposure that I've found in the United States.

Even after coming to the United States, I had to work to create my own breaks. One of the best moves I made was to network with others who shared my passion for speaking and inspiring others. Studies have shown that most people learn about job openings through their professional networks of friends and co-workers. As with most other types of opportunities, you hear about them on the grapevine long before other sources have the news. Whether you are looking for love, a job, an investment, a place to volunteer, or a venue to share your talents, you can make your own breaks by joining professional groups, local clubs, the Chamber of Commerce, or church, charitable, and service organizations. The Internet is tailor-made for making helpful connections, with social networking sites such as Twitter, Facebook, LinkedIn, and Plaxo. The wider your circle, the greater your chances for finding an open door to your dream.

You shouldn't limit yourself to just those individuals, organizations, and Web sites related to your field of interest. Everybody knows somebody who knows somebody. So seek out anyone who is passionate and committed to a dream, even if theirs is entirely different from yours. I love passionate people because they attract opportunities like mighty magnets.

On the other hand, if you are hanging with a crowd of folks who don't share your dreams, or your commitment to bettering your life, I'd advise you to find a new group of friends. Those who hang in bars, nightclubs, or video arcades rarely soar.

If you aren't attracting the sort of offers and options you aspire to, maybe you need to find higher ground through higher education. If you can't win acceptance to a college or university, work your way up through community college or a tech school. More scholarships and financial aid programs are available than you might imagine, so don't let the costs discourage you. If you've already earned a degree, you may want to upgrade to a master's or doctorate program, or join professional organizations, online communities, or Internet forums and chat rooms for people in your field. If the breaks aren't coming your way, then you need to get to the place where they can find you, or you can find them.

OPPORTUNE TIME

Albert Einstein said that in the middle of every difficulty lies opportunity. The recent recession has left millions of people unemployed. Countless others have lost their homes and their savings. What good can come of hard times?

Among the major brand companies that started up during recessions and depressions are Hewlett Packard, Wrigley, UPS, Microsoft, Symantec, Toys "R" Us, Zippo, and Domino's Pizza. The founders of these companies were looking for new and better ways to serve customers because previous models had failed during downturns. They seized the moment to create their own vision for doing business.

Without a doubt, the recession of 2006–9 had a profound and

lingering impact that hurt many, many families and businesses. But many of the people cast out by corporations and longtime employers responded by starting their own businesses, going back to school for advanced degrees, or finally pursuing their passion in life, whether it was opening a bakery, starting a gardening service, forming a band, or writing a book.

Among those laid off or terminated in the recession were thousands and thousands of journalists. The downturn hit their industry especially hard because it occurred just as newspapers around the world were losing their lucrative classified ad business to online services like craigslist. It's been interesting to see how former journalists, who pride themselves on their resourcefulness and creativity, have responded. Several I know have launched new careers in public relations, nonprofit ventures, and Web-based media and blogs. One of my favorites is the former editor who left his shrinking California newspaper and became vice president of a booming crisis-management company that crafts "bankruptcy communications" for other businesses in decline. This is the Taking Lemons and Making Lemonade philosophy, which is really all about shifting your focus from moaning about the problem to finding a creative solution. You have to be flexible, determined, and ready to turn a potentially negative situation into a positive situation. One of the big American retail chains teaches its sales staff to view customer complaints as invitations for building better relationships with store patrons.

It's a matter of reframing. I do it whenever my schedule hits a snag by reminding myself that "God does not waste His time, so He doesn't waste mine either." In other words, it all works out for the good. I truly believe that, and you should too. When you buy into that philosophy, stand back. I've seen it proven true time and time again.

ON THE CLOCK

A few years ago I was flying with my caregiver across the country. At one airport our flight was delayed (no surprise), and when we finally were on the plane and taxiing from the departure gate, I looked out the window and saw smoke coming from the engine.

A fire truck came roaring up. The firefighters jumped out and sprayed foam on the engine to put out the blaze. *Due to a small fire in the engine,* the passengers were told, *we will be conducting an emergency evacuation of this plane.*

Well, all right, I thought. Fire in the engine was not good, but being on the ground when the "small fire" broke out was a plus. When it was announced that our flight would be delayed another two hours, many of my fellow passengers complained loudly and bitterly. I was irritated but glad we had been spared a possible mid-flight emergency, or so I told myself.

Still, I struggled a bit to remain positive since we were on a tight schedule. *Remember, God doesn't waste time,* I told myself. Then came yet another announcement: They'd lined up another plane at another gate to take us immediately. *Good news!*

We hurried to the new departure gate, boarded yet another plane, and settled in for the flight. I was relieved until I noticed that the woman sitting next to me was quietly weeping.

"Is there something I can do?" I asked.

She explained that she was flying to visit her fifteen-year-old daughter, who was in danger of dying after a routine surgery had gone terribly wrong. I did my best to comfort the mother. We talked for nearly the entire flight. I even drew a smile from her after she told me she was nervous about flying.

"You can hold my hand if you like," I teased.

When we landed at our destination, the mother thanked me for comforting her. I told her I was grateful that I'd ended up seated next to her on the plane after so many delays and gate changes.

God had not wasted my time that day. He knew what He was doing. He put me next to that woman to help her with her fears and grief. The more I thought about that day, the more grateful I was for the chance to offer this woman a sympathetic ear.

CREATIVE VISION

A lost loved one, a broken relationship, a financial setback, or an illness can break you if you let grief and despair overtake you. One way to fight through those challenges is to stay alert for what rises up even when life seems to be taking you down.

I met the photographer Glennis Siverson on the set of *The Butterfly Circus*. Though she lives in Orlando, Glennis had come to California to serve as the set photographer at the invitation of the directors and her friends the Weigels. Glennis is an award-winning photographer whose work is commissioned by magazines, corporations, newspapers, and Web sites. She also does portrait and nature photography. She loves photography. It is her passion.

But for more than twenty years, Glennis worked in the human resources field for big companies. She lost her "safe and secure" job in the recession. Glennis took that kick in the pants and used the forward momentum to pursue her passion. She became a full-time photographer.

"I decided it was now or never!" she said.

Great story, right? Glennis is a real-life example of someone who took a potentially negative event and used it as an opportunity to create an even better life.

Terrific! Wonderful!

But there's more. You see, Glennis, the award-winning photographer, can hardly see. She is legally blind.

"Ever since I was a child I have had poor eyesight," she said. "I got glasses at age five and my vision kept getting worse. Then around 1995 I was diagnosed with corneal disease. The cornea is misshapen and degenerates. It got to the point that I couldn't see out of my left eye. Since I had extremely severe nearsightedness, it was past the threshold to get Lasik surgery. My only option was a cornea transplant."

In 2004 Glennis underwent that surgery. Her doctor had told her that it would correct the vision in her left eye to 20/40 without glasses or contacts. "But everything that could go wrong pretty much did—short of losing my eye," she said. "The operation made my vision worse. I also got glaucoma as a result. My vision worsened in my left eye, and then, unrelated to the operation, I had a hemorrhage on the retina of my right eye. So I have a blind spot on it."

Laid off from her job of twenty years, and all but blinded by failed surgery and a hemorrhaged retina, Glennis could not be blamed for despairing and giving up. You might expect her to grow bitter and angry.

Instead, she was grateful to soar higher and farther. "I don't think of myself as *disabled*. I think of myself as *enabled*, because being nearly blind has made me a better photographer," she said.

She can no longer see fine details, but instead of feeling deprived, she is grateful that she is free not to obsess about the little things anymore.

"Prior to losing most of my eyesight, if I was doing portrait photography, I was focused on every strand of hair and every angle of the person's body. My work looked stiff because I was so focused on composition. But now my approach is pretty much a gut reaction. I feel it. I see it, and I shoot it. My work is more instinctual, and I interact with people and surroundings much more.

Glennis said her photographs now are flawed but are more artful, more compelling. "One gal actually cried when she saw my images of her because she felt I'd captured her so well," she said. "I had never moved anyone emotionally before."

Since she lost much of her eyesight, Glennis has won ten international awards for her portrait and landscape photography.

One of her photos was selected from sixteen thousand entries for an exhibition of just 111 works. She's had photos selected for four exhibitions at the Center for Fine Art Photography in Fort Collins, Colorado.

Her blindness would never have allowed Glennis to continue her job in human resources, but many great artists such as Monet and Beethoven thrived despite disabilities because they used them as opportunities to explore their art in new and fresh ways. Grateful, Glennis told me that her favorite Bible verse is now "We live by faith, not by sight."

"That literally is my life now. I've had to make adjustments, sure. I worry about being totally blind. It's been very, very scary. There is no manual for this."

She is on a new path, but instead of seeing it as a disruption in her life, she views it as a gift. "I'd been very controlling before. Now I try to live day to day and enjoy each moment," she said. "I also try to be grateful that I have a roof over my head and I'm alive and the sun is shining and I don't worry about tomorrow because we never know what tomorrow will bring."

Glennis is a great lady, who embraces opportunity, don't you agree? She inspires me, and I hope she inspires you to look for ways to advance your dreams, choose them wisely, and then act upon them when your heart says "go."

ELEVEN

The Ridiculous Rules

We were halfway through a five-city tour of Indonesia where I was speaking thirty-five times in nine days. I should have been dog tired. Sometimes on these manically busy stretches I rev up and can't settle down. We were headed to Java, and just as we were boarding the plane from Jakarta to Semarang, a rush of energy swept over me.

Five people were traveling with me, including my caregiver Vaughan, who is a big, strong, fun-loving guy. The female flight attendants were quite impressed with him as we boarded the plane, and we were teasing back and forth. They let us on first because I have to get out of my wheelchair and walk through the plane to my seat. As I headed down the aisle of the plane with Vaughan behind me, I suddenly had this urge to try something crazy that I'd thought about doing for a while.

"Vaughan, quick, before anyone else comes aboard—lift me up and see if I fit in the overhead baggage compartment!"

We'd often joked about doing this. A few days earlier I'd had Vaughan place me inside the metal frame at the departure for seeing if your luggage will fit in the overhead compartment. I easily fit, so they started calling me "the Carry-on Kid."

The overhead compartment was quite high, and I wasn't sure anyone could lift my seventy-four pounds up there, but Vaughan had no trouble. He hoisted me up and gently placed me on my side in the compartment as if I were a Vuitton instead of a Vujicic.

"Okay, now close the door," I said, "and let's wait for the other passengers to come on board."

Vaughan tucked a pillow under my head and snapped the door shut, leaving me perched above the seats. The flight attendants saw what we were up to and cracked up with laughter. We were all snickering like schoolkids, so I wasn't sure we would pull off this prank. But the other passengers came up the ramp, unaware of the stowaway in the overhead.

My crew and the flight attendants could hardly contain themselves when an older gentleman came down the aisle and reached up to put his bag in my compartment. He opened the door—and nearly jumped through the roof of the airplane.

I popped my head out. "Sir, I don't believe you even knocked!"

Luckily, he was a good-natured bloke, and we all had a nice belly laugh. Then while still perched in the overhead, I had to pose for a couple hundred pictures with him, other passengers, and the flight attendants. Of course Vaughan kept threatening to leave me up there, warning that "some items may shift in flight."

UNRULY FOR THE ROAD

In the first ten chapters I've offered you encouragement and guidance about finding your purpose, being hopeful, believing in yourself, maintaining a good attitude, acting with courage, practicing resilience, mastering change, forming empowering relationships, and acting upon opportunities that move you closer to your dreams.

Now I want you to get a little crazy. Just like me.

I'm being ridiculous, of course. In fact, ridiculous is exactly what I want you to be too. I am the creator of the Ridiculous Rules, which hold that every living, breathing person on the planet should be committed to doing something ridiculous at least once a day, whether it's risking looking ridiculous to pursue a dream or simply having ridiculous fun.

My Ridiculous Rules spring from one of my favorite quotes: "Imperfection is beauty, madness is genius and it's better to be absolutely ridiculous than absolutely boring."

Now the alleged author of that intriguing quotation is not exactly one of my role models, but I think the late actress Marilyn Monroe was on to something when she uttered it. Naturally, I agree that imperfection is beauty, why wouldn't I? You can't argue either with the fact that madness is genius—in the sense that anyone who takes risks is bound to be considered a madman by some and a genius by others. And yes, I do think it's better to be absolutely ridiculous than to be absolutely boring.

You can master every other lesson in this book, but if you aren't willing to take some risks or dare to be called crazy by those who doubt your genius, then you likely will never achieve all that you dream of achieving. And for your sake and the planet's, please dare to be playful too. Don't forget to laugh at yourself and kick up your heels now and then so that you enjoy the journey.

I'm as guilty as anyone of falling into an overscheduled, all-work-and-not-enough-play lifestyle. I was determined to become a successful evangelist and a motivational speaker. To hone my speaking skills, I hit the road, jumping on every speaking invitation I could line up. After eight dizzying years of nonstop touring and speaking, I've become more selective. I need more balance.

We easily become trapped in the "someday" mentality.

Someday I'll have all the money I need so I can enjoy life.

Someday I'll be able to spend more time with my family.

Someday I'll have time to relax and do what I love doing.

With the Ridiculous Rules, I encourage you to embrace your freedom to romp on two fronts.

Number one is Ridiculous Risk: Be willing to blow past the doubters and the naysayers and make a leap to live your dreams. Some may say you are being ridiculous. Your response should be: *Why, yes I am!* Doing what you love may seem ridiculous to people who don't share your vision or your passion. You can't let their ridicule rid you of your dream. Instead, use it to ride it all the way to the top!

Number two is Ridiculous Fun: Take time to enjoy your life and your loved ones. Laugh, love, and have ridiculous fun so others can share the joy. If you think life is serious, imagine death! In this blessed life be as serious as you need to be, but take the opportunity to be just as playful as you can be too.

RIDICULOUS RISK

Helen Keller, who lost both her sight and hearing in childhood but became a renowned activist and author, said that there is no such thing as a secure life. "It does not exist in nature . . . Life is either a daring adventure or nothing." Risk, then, is not just part of life. It *is* life. The place between your comfort zone and your dream is where life takes place. It's the high-anxiety zone, but it's also where you discover who you are. Karl Wallenda, patriarch of the legendary high-wire-walking family, nailed it when he said: "Being on the tightrope is living; everything else is waiting."

Every sky diver, paraglider, and baby Kookaburra bird knows that the first walk to the edge is scary, but they have to go there if they want to fly. Face it—every day could be your last, so it's a roll of the dice just to get out of bed. You can't be a winner unless you're willing to face defeat. You can't even stand without risking a fall.

My day-to-day life has been a dicey business since birth. There were doubts as to whether I'd ever be able to support or care for myself. My parents had double trouble because their limbless child was also a thrill seeker. I was forever putting myself in danger because I couldn't bear to just sit around and be the kid in the corner. I skateboarded. I played soccer. I swam. I surfed. I threw my poor body around like an unguided missile. It was ridiculous!

DIVING IN

In the fall of 2009 I tried something that I'd once been told was way too dangerous for me: I went scuba diving in the ocean. As you probably can guess, I had a blast. It was like flying but with softer landings. I'd tried to scuba about three years earlier, but the instructor would only let me paddle around the pool in scuba gear. I think he was more worried about his insurance than my safety. He was afraid he'd have to explain why that strange guy named Nick was carried off by a shark looking for a bite-size bloke.

This time my instructor, Felipe, had a more open mind. He is the dive instructor on a little island off Colombia, South America. I'd been invited to speak there by the owners of the gorgeous Punta Faro Resort on tiny Mucura Island, a national park, just off Cartagena. Felipe's only question to me when I showed up for a scuba lesson was "Can you swim?"

Once I proved seaworthy, Felipe gave me a quick resort scuba course. We worked out some sign language so I could communicate with him under water: by moving my shoulders or my head, I could let him know I needed help. Then he took me out for a test run just off the beach, where we practiced a bit, tried our underwater signals, and checked the equipment.

"Okay, I think you're ready for the reef," he said.

Felipe gripped me around the waist and, using his flippers, swam with me down to the reef surrounded by a dazzling rainbow of marine life. Then he let me go, floating above me while I explored the reef. He had to rescue me only once when a five-foot-long moray eel popped out of a crevice in the coral. I'd read that these carnivorous eels have nasty teeth covered with bacteria, so I signaled Felipe to tow me to a friendlier section of the reef. I didn't want to become Nick sushi.

The experience opened my eyes to a whole new world. You may

wonder whether it was worth the ridiculous risk. Undoubtedly, yes! Stepping out of your place of comfort opens the possibility for stretching and growing. Surely there is some daring move you've wanted to dive into? I encourage you to do it, test the waters, and take your life to a new level, even if it is under water. Swim with the dolphins. Soar with the eagles. Climb a mountain. Spelunk a cave! Be *ridic* like Nick!

Now, there is a difference between ridiculous risk and just plain stupid risk. Stupid risks are just that, too crazy to contemplate. You should never take a risk in which you could lose more than you could win. Ridiculous risk, however, is taking a chance that looks or sounds crazier than it really is because:

1. You've prepared yourself.

2. You have reduced the risk as much as possible.

3. You have a backup plan if things go wrong.

RISK TYPES

I learned about risk mitigation while studying financial planning and economics in university. In the business world as in life, it is generally conceded that you can't avoid risk entirely, but you can manage or minimize it by measuring the depth of the muck before you wade in—no matter what sort of muck you are wading into.

There are two types of risk in life: the danger of trying and the danger of not trying. That is to say, there is always risk, no matter how you may try to avoid it or protect yourself. Let's say you are interested in dating someone. It's a gamble just to call and ask the person out. You might be turned down. But what if you don't try? After all, this wonderful person might say yes. You might hit it off and live happily ever after. Remember that you have virtually no chance of living "happily ever after" unless you put yourself out there. Isn't that worth a tumble, mate?

You will lose now and then. You will fail. But the glory lies in getting back up again and again until you succeed!

To live, you must be willing to reach and stretch. To live well, you must learn to control the odds by knowing the upside and downside before you make a move. You can't control everything that happens to you or around you, so focus on what you can control, assess every possibility you can assess, and then make a decision.

Sometimes your heart and your gut will tell you to take a chance even when the odds of success look bad on paper. You may fail. You may win. But I doubt that you will ever look back with regret that you tried. I consider myself a business entrepreneur as well as a public speaker and evangelist. I've had several business and real estate ventures over the years. I've read many books about entrepreneurs, and there is always a section on risk. Despite the image of entrepreneurs as "risk takers," successful entrepreneurs aren't really good at taking risks; they are good at controlling and minimizing risks and then moving forward, even when they know some risk remains.

MY RIDICULOUS RULES

To help you deal with the risks you'll face in your life, I've put together Nick's Ridiculous Rules for Managing Risk. Read them at your own . . . well, you know.

1. Test the waters.

An ancient African proverb says no one tests the depth of the river with both feet. If you are considering a new relationship, a move to another city, a new job, or even a new color for the living room, do a little test before making a big move. Don't rush in without a good sense of what you are getting into.

2. Go with what you know.

This doesn't mean you should never try new experiences or new people; it simply means that you can lower the odds by doing your homework. Once you think you have a handle on the upside, downside, and every aspect of an opportunity, you should have the confidence to make a move. Even if you don't know it all, you should know what you don't know—and sometimes that's good enough.

3. Check the timer.

Often you can greatly improve the odds by waiting for the right time to make your move. You wouldn't want to start a new ice-cream business in the dead of winter, would you? My first offer to enter the movie business just wasn't for me, but a few months later the role was perfect and the timing was right. Sometimes patience can pay off. Don't be afraid to sleep on it. Write it down before you go to bed, and then read it again in the morning. It's amazing how different it can appear when you let it sit overnight. I have done this many times. Always consider your timing and whether there might be a better time before you make a move on the steep edge of opportunity.

4. Get a second opinion.

Sometimes we take bigger chances than we should because we're so convinced that we absolutely must do a certain thing right now. If you find yourself rushing into tricky territory, take a couple steps back, call a friend or mentor you trust, and ask for help in assessing the situation, because your emotions may be outrunning your good sense. I go to my uncle Batta here and to my father in Australia. There is wisdom in a council of many. If the stakes are high, you don't have to be the Lone Ranger.

5. Prepare for the unseen consequences.

There are always, I repeat *always*, unseen consequences for our actions, especially those that push the envelope. You can never foresee all the repercussions, so you should do your best to consider every angle and then prepare yourself for the unexpected. When I do a business plan, I overestimate costs and underestimate my profit to create a buffer, just in case the business doesn't progress as well as I hope it will. If all goes well, it never hurts to have the extra money.

RIDICULOUS FUN

Don't even pretend that you haven't stood waiting for your baggage in an airport and contemplated leaping onto the carousel to ride wherever it takes you in Luggage Land. Of course, being ridiculous, I did it.

We were in Africa on a speaking tour. When we arrived at the airport, I grew bored waiting for our luggage, so I told my caregiver Kyle that I wanted to go on a carousel ride.

He looked at me like *Dude, have you gone mad as a cut snake?*

But Kyle came through. He hoisted me up and plopped me down next to a nice big Samsonite. Off I went with the rest of the bags and cases. I rode the wild carousel through the terminal, making like a statue, wearing my sunglasses, and drawing shocked stares, pointed fingers, and nervous laughter from the other travelers, who weren't sure if I was (a) a real person, or (b) the world's most hand-some duffle.

Finally I rode the carousel up to the little door leading into the backroom loading area, where I was greeted by the African bag men laughing and smiling at the crazy Aussie on a joy ride.

"God bless you!" they said, cheering me on.

The baggage workers understood that sometimes even grown-ups have to hitch a ride on the carousel. Youth isn't wasted on children. They enjoy every minute of it. You and I should do whatever we can to keep that youthful joy alive. If your life is too predictable, don't go postal. Take a ridiculous ride back to whatever it was that gave you joy as a child. Jump on a trampoline. Saddle up a pony. Give adulthood a rest.

I encourage you to use up every second. Every now and then I cut loose and do something just for fun. I encourage you to live the same way, in vigorous pursuit of all the wonders that God has given us on this earth.

To live ridiculously is to live at the convergence of hope and possibility, embracing God's purpose and His plan. The second part of the Ridiculous Rules, then, is all about having ridiculous fun, defying expectations, and exceeding limitations. It's about enjoying the ride, embracing the blessings, and always pushing not just to live but to enjoy your life to the fullest.

In my speeches, I often stand poised right at the edge of my speaking platform, teetering as if I'm about to take a tumble. I tell my audiences that living on the edge isn't such a bad way to go when you have faith in yourself and in your Creator. That's not just talk. I push myself in every aspect of my life, both work and play. The most ridiculously good feeling comes over me when work and play become one. I encourage you to go for that feeling too.

STUNTMAN

When I accepted my first acting role in *The Butterfly Circus*, I did not anticipate that I would do my own stunt work. But then, who better to do my stunts than me? It's not like there are a lot of professional stuntmen with no arms and no legs looking for work.

I was game. If my fellow Aussie Russell Crowe can do his own movie dives, why shouldn't I? Then again, Russell has never been tossed around like a beach ball by George the Strong Man. The real stuntman and actor Matt Allmen played that burly character in *The Butterfly Circus*. In one key scene in the film, Matt, playing George, picks me up and throws me into a small pond. Matt was very nervous about that scene. I should have been more nervous myself.

We filmed it in a natural pool in a real creek in the San Gabriel Mountains in California's High Desert. The water was cold, but that wasn't the worst of it. In the scene we filmed, I accidentally fall into the creek's pool and everyone fears that I've drowned, but I of course pop up, showing off my swimming ability.

George the Strong Man gets so excited that I'm alive that he picks me up and throws me, nearly drowning me himself.

Matt was afraid he'd hurt me by throwing me too far or too hard. He was a little timid in the first few takes because the water was only about five feet deep. The director, Joshua Weigel, encouraged him to give me a stronger toss, and I came flying out of Matt's arms like a torpedo! Afraid I would smack into the rock bottom, I arched my back, which saved me. This time there was no acting involved when I popped back up out of the water. Everyone on the set was truly joyful when I came up for air, especially Matt.

Even riskier, though, were my high-diving scenes, in which I had to be hoisted about three stories in a harness in front of a "green screen." Hanging over the set by a few straps made for some scary moments. Of course, the risks of my film work were mitigated by professional stunt coordinators on the set. They took care of the safety nets and rigging so even the scariest parts were fun.

The truth is that taking a moderate physical risk now and then, whether it's rock climbing, surfing, or snowboarding, can pump you up and make you feel more alive. Children and adults often incorporate risk into their favorite forms of play, even if it's just the risk of appearing ridiculous while unleashing your inner eight year old.

PLAY FOR LIFE

Dr. Stuart Brown, a psychiatrist and founder of the National Institute for Play, says that we are hardwired to play and that to neglect our natural playful impulses can be as dangerous as avoiding sleep. Dr. Brown studied Death Row inmates and serial killers and found that nearly all of them had childhoods that lacked normal play patterns. He says the opposite of play is not work, it is depression, so play might well be considered a survival skill.

Risky, rough-and-tumble play helps children and adults develop their social, cognitive, emotional, and physical skills, according to Dr. Brown, who believes we should even try to incorporate work and play rather than just setting aside time for recreation.

I've known of men who spent their youths chasing recognition and wealth, only to hit their later years and realize that they had reached the end of a journey that they did not enjoy. Don't let that happen to you. Do what you need to do to survive, but do what you love as often as possible too!

It's scary how you can get so caught up in daily routines and the struggle to make a living that you neglect the quality of your day-to-day life. Balance isn't something you achieve "someday." So don't forget to have some ridiculous fun by enjoying whatever playful activity so absorbs you that you lose track of time and place.

Studies have shown that being "lost" or totally engaged in your favorite activity, whether it's playing Monopoly, painting a landscape, or running a marathon, may just be as close to true happiness as we can get on this earth. I often fall into that sort of "flow" state when I fish, which is my favorite form of relaxing play.

My parents first took me when I was just six years old. My mum gave me a hand line with corn niblets as bait. She threw it into the water, and I held on to the line with my toes. I was a determined tyke. I figured I could outwait the fish. Sooner or later they'd have to take a bite of my corn because I wasn't leaving until I hooked a whopper.

My strategy worked. A two-foot fish finally went after my niblet, probably because he was tired of my little shadow hovering over the water. When the monster took my bait and ran with it, he pulled the fishing line through my toes and it hurt like crazy. Rather than let go of the fish, I came up with an ingenious move. I sat on the line, which then burned my bum when the big fish kept pulling on it.

"I've got a fish. Oh, my bum hurts. But I've got a fish!" I screamed.

My mum and dad and cousins came running to help me pull in the whopper, one that was about the same length as me. Mine was the biggest fish caught all day, and it was worth every bit of my pain. After that, I was hooked on fishing for life.

I no longer use just a hand-held fishing line. I mastered the rod and reel so I wouldn't suffer any more bum burns. If a fish bites, I'm strong enough to hold the rod between my shoulder and chin. I cast by holding the line in my teeth and releasing at just the right moment. Yes, it's true, I floss and fish at the same time!

MUSICALLY INCLINED

If you think fishing is an outrageous pastime for me, just think how people respond when I tell them I was not only a drummer in my school band but a conductor too! It's true, though. I've got the beat, mate. I mastered the rare musical art of hymnal percussion at a young age. Every Sunday night at church I'd set up rows of hymnals of varied thickness. I'd pound out a beat on the hymn books with my foot while the church choir sang. I come from a long line of avid drummers, including my cousin Ian Pasula, who was the first drummer in the church band. I had such a natural ability to keep a beat that a couple of my uncles and their church friends kicked in to buy me a Roland drum machine. This amplified wonder transformed me into a one-man, no-limbed percussion orchestra. I started with just the snare drum and bass drum and later progressed to incorporating the closed and open high hats.

The church's pianist, organist, and drummers would join in and make me feel part of the band. I still play a newer version of the drum machine, which I've upgraded with a Mac Keys program, where I can use it as a synthesizer and even play a guitar electronically. Music is a balm for my soul. Whether listening or playing, I can lose myself for hours in waves of sound.

My love of music was nurtured in jazz ensembles and high school jazz bands. Perhaps the musical highlight of my life so far came when I quite literally took my entire high school orchestra on my shoulders. Now there's a job you'd never expect someone like me to take in hand. *Reeediculous*, right?

Well, our music teacher was having health problems, and she couldn't make our rehearsals, so I volunteered to be the conductor for our sixty-piece orchestra. I knew all the songs we were playing, so I stood in front of our huge group of student musicians and led them by waving my shoulders around. I'll go out on a limb here and say that they sounded ridiculously good that day.

A RIDICULOUS CONCLUSION

Most of us have little clue as to what God has planned for us each day, each month, year, or lifetime. But each of us has the capacity to add our own flourishes, to pursue our purpose, our passion, and our pleasures with reckless abandon and ridiculous enthusiasm. In this chapter alone, I've recounted my adventures as an airplane carry-on and an airport carousel rider, as a scuba diver and a stuntman, as a fisherman, a drummer, and an orchestra conductor. My question to you now is: If imperfect me can have that much ridiculous fun, if I can push the limits and enjoy life so fully, what about you?

Live to glorify God, and don't leave an ounce of energy, a trace of your uniqueness, behind. Dare to be ridiculous, and you will be ridiculously happy.

TWELVE

Make Giving Your Mission

When I was twenty, I decided to go to South Africa on a two-week speaking tour arranged by someone I'd never met. My mum and dad were not enthused because they were concerned about my safety and health, and about the costs involved. Can you imagine that? John Pingo had seen one of my first videos and made it his mission to lure me to speak to the neediest people in the poorest regions of his country. On his own he set up a series of appearances for me at congregations, schools, and orphanages through his network of Doxa Deo churches.

John wrote, called, and e-mailed, begging me to come to his country. His persistence and enthusiasm triggered something in me. When I was growing up and sometimes tortured over my circumstances and my future, the one action other than prayer that seemed to bring me relief was to reach out and do something for another person. The more I dwelled on my own challenges, the worse I felt, but when I changed my focus to serving the needs of someone else, it lifted my spirits and helped me understand that no one suffers alone.

Whether you have a lot or a little to offer, just remember that small acts of kindness can be just as powerful as big donations. If you make a difference in just one life, you've done a great service, because simple kindness can start a chain reaction of similar actions, resulting in your effort's initial results becoming magnified many times. How many times have you had someone do something nice for you and then, feeling grateful, you turn around and do a kindness for someone else? I believe it is part of our God-given nature to respond in this manner.

Earlier I told you how a simple kind comment from a girl in my school infused me with confidence at a critical point in my life when I had been feeling useless and unwanted. She gave me a boost that made me think maybe I did have something to offer, and now I seek to provide inspiration to those in need worldwide while spreading the word of God's love. That girl's simple kindness to me has been magnified many, many times over.

So if you say that you would do more if you had more, I encourage you to simply do what you can now and every day. Money isn't the only contribution you can make. Whatever God has given you, share it in ways to benefit others. If you have carpentry or other trade skills, offer them to your church, to Habitat for Humanity, or to the victims of disasters in Haiti and other needy places. Whether it's sewing or singing, accounting or auto repair, there are plenty of ways you can multiply your talents.

A high school student from Hong Kong recently e-mailed my Web site, demonstrating how we can all make a difference no matter how old, how rich, or how poor.

> I live a very fortunate life, but even still there were times when I none-theless felt useless and frightened. I was scared entering my high school years because of stories I'd heard about how the older students might treat you. Then on my first day of school, I joined the other students in my Humanities in Action classroom and I had a great teacher who taught us to no longer see ourselves as a class but a family.
>
> Over time we learned so many things. We were introduced to important events in other parts of the world, such as the 1994 genocide in Rwanda and the current Genocide in Darfur, Sudan. My class and I came to feel something that we had never felt before: Passion. We had a passion to understand and help what was happening to the people in Darfur. Even

though people wouldn't expect much from 14-year-old kids, we found a way of showing the world how we could make a difference.

We put on a performance in which we showed the audience what was happening in Darfur. We found a passion that ignited our souls and spirit. Because of this we were able to do the unexpected and raised enough money to send essential supplies to help people in Darfur.

Those are wise words from a young person, aren't they? The passion to serve others may be the greatest gift God can bestow. I'm sure the people in Darfur who benefited from the supplies were grateful for every single item, big or small. The awesome power of God is reflected in the fact that if we want to do something for others, our availability is every bit as important as our capability. God works through us when we reach out for others. Once you make yourself available for good works, guess whose capabilities you can rely on? God's! The Bible says, "I can do all things through Christ who strengthens me."

Whatever you want for yourself, do it for others. If you make even small acts of compassion a daily habit, you will feel empowered and liberated from your own hurts and disappointments. You shouldn't expect to benefit from being generous or supportive to others, but good deeds can lead to surprising rewards.

I'm an advocate of unconditional generosity because it honors God and multiplies His blessings. Yet I also believe that when you do unto others, blessings come to you as well. So if you don't have a friend, be a friend. If you are having a bad day, make someone else's day. If your feelings are hurt, heal those of another.

You never know how much of a difference you can make in this world simply by performing a small act of kindness. Small ripples can set huge waves in motion. The classmate who saw that I was feeling down after being teased and told me that I was looking good not only soothed my hurt feelings, she lit a spark that ignited my career and my mission to reach out to others worldwide.

A PASSION FOR REACHING OUT

Don't worry about how much you can do to benefit others. Just reach out and know that small acts of kindness multiply and are strengthened beyond anything you might imagine. Like the student from Hong Kong, I became more and more passionate about traveling to South Africa the more I thought about it and the more I heard from John Pingo.

I prayed about the proposed trip for three weeks. After that, I really felt that I had a calling to go. I wanted to offer inspiration without limits, and this seemed like a good first step toward a worldwide ministry. I knew very little about South Africa, and I had never traveled that far without my parents. My dad did have friends who lived there, and after he spoke with them, he wasn't reassured. They reported that violent crime was a serious problem and that travelers were often attacked, robbed, and even killed.

"It's not a safe place to go, Nick," my father said. "You don't even know this John Pingo. Why would you trust him to take you all over that country?"

My mum and dad have very few gray hairs, which is surprising given some of my adventures as a strong-willed young man. But like all parents, they are very protective of me. Given my disabilities, they felt they had all the more reason to be concerned about my safety. But I yearned to make my way, to follow my calling and get on with my career as an evangelist and inspirational speaker.

When I raised the prospect of the South Africa trip, their initial concern was for my welfare and financial stability. I'd just bought my first house with my earnings, and they felt I should be paying off my debts instead of gallivanting around the globe.

Their concerns increased dramatically when I also revealed to them that (1) while I was in South Africa, I intended to give away more than $20,000 of my life savings to orphanages, and (2) I wanted to take my little brother with me.

Looking back from my parents' perspective today, I can better appreciate how worrying it must have been for them. But I was determined. The Bible says, "If anyone has material possessions and sees his brother in need but has no pity on him, how can the love of God be in him?" I wanted to act on my faith by serving others. Though I am disabled, I felt enabled by my faith, and I felt that it was time to serve my purpose.

I still had to convince my parents that I would be safe. Even my brother was not all that enthused about going with me at first. In fact, when I asked him, initially he refused because of the reports of violence and "I don't want to be eaten by a lion." I kept pushing and prodding him, tried to explain the situation about lions. I'd recruited two cousins to go; one had to drop out. Aaron then felt it was his duty to go and help me make the trip. My parents and I prayed about this journey, and eventually they gave their blessing to go forward with it. They were still concerned, but they trusted God would look after us.

SERVING THE WORLD

When we arrived in South Africa after a long flight, our host was waiting for us at the airport as promised, but for some reason I'd pictured John Pingo to be an older man, maybe not as old as my parents but at least in his thirties.

He was nineteen years old! That was a year younger than I was at the time.

Maybe this wasn't such a good idea, I thought when we met at the airport. Fortunately, John proved to be a very mature and capable bloke, who opened my eyes to more poverty and need than I'd ever witnessed. He told me how he had been inspired by my life story when he saw my video, but I came to realize that his story was every bit as compelling, and his dedication to his faith humbled me.

He grew up on a livestock farm in the Republic of the Orange

Free State in southern South Africa. He'd run with a bad crowd earlier in life, but he'd become an avid Christian and was now the owner of a small trucking company. He was grateful to God for helping him change his life and for blessing him.

John was so determined to have me speak words of faith and inspiration around his country that he'd sold his own car to raise enough money for our tour of churches, schools, orphanages, and prisons. Then he'd borrowed his aunt's blue van to haul me to speaking engagements in Cape Town, Pretoria, Johannesburg, and all points in between.

It was a crazy schedule, and we often went with just four or five hours of sleep each day. But this trip introduced me to people, places, and things that changed my life forever. It helped me realize what I wanted to do with the rest of my life: to share my message of encouragement and faith around the globe.

Aaron and I thought we'd seen a bit growing up in Australia and living for a short time in California. But on this trip we realized we were babes in these woods. That realization really sank in when we left the airport and were driving through Johannesburg. Aaron looked out his window at an intersection and saw a sign that terrified him: "Smash and Grab Area."

Aaron looked at our driver. "John, what does that sign mean?"

"Oh, that means this is an area where they will smash your car windows, grab your things out of the car, and run off," said John.

We locked the doors and began scanning all around us. We noted that many people lived in homes surrounded by high concrete walls with barbed-wire fencing at the top. Several people we met in the first couple days told of being mugged or robbed, but eventually we found that South Africa was no more dangerous than many other regions where poverty and crime are concerns.

In fact, Aaron and I both fell in love with South Africa and its people. Despite all this nation's problems, we found South Africans to be wonderful, filled with hope and joy despite their circumstances. We'd never seen such depths of poverty and despair, nor such inexplicable joy and unyielding faith, as we found there.

The orphanages were both heart-wrenching and inspiring. We visited one orphanage dedicated to rescuing abandoned children who had been left in trash cans and on park benches. Most of them were sick and suffering from malnutrition. They affected us so much that we returned the next day with pizza, soft drinks, toys, soccer balls, and other simple gifts. The children were ecstatic about them.

But we also saw children with open wounds from flesh-eating bacteria, children and adults dying of AIDS, and families living day to day in search of food and clean water to drink. To see that up close, to smell the sickness and death hovering over human beings in agony, and to know that all I could do was pray over them to comfort them, was such an eye-opening experience. I had never seen such poverty and suffering. It was so much worse than anything I've ever endured, and it made my life seem pampered by comparison. I was overwhelmed with conflicting feelings: compassion that made me want to leap into action and save everyone I could, and anger at the existence of such suffering and its seeming unchangeability.

Our father often spoke of his childhood in Serbia, having only a piece of bread and a little water and sugar for dinner at night. His father, my grandfather, had been a barber by trade. He had worked in a government salon, but when he refused to join the Communist Party, he was forced out. It was difficult for him to operate his own shop because of constant pressure from the Communists. The family had to move once or twice a year so that my grandfather, whose faith prohibited him from bearing arms, could avoid being drafted into the military. When he contracted tuberculosis and could no longer work at his trade, my grandmother had to support their six children with work as a seamstress.

My father's stories of his family's struggles carried new mean-

ing for me after I witnessed poverty and hunger up close in South
Africa; now I'd seen anguish in the eyes of dying mothers and heard
their children screaming because of their aching, empty stomachs.
We visited slums where families lived in tiny tin sheds no bigger
than storage rooms, with newspapers for insulation and no running water. I spoke at a prison where the inmates filled the chapel
and a courtyard outside it. We learned that many of the prisoners
were still awaiting trial and that the only crime of many was to
owe money to someone with the power to have them arrested. We
met one prisoner who'd been sentenced to serve ten years because
he owed $200. That day the prisoners sang for us, and their voices
soared with amazing joy in such a desolate place.

MAKING A DIFFERENCE

I'd gone to South Africa as a young man full of himself, sure that I
could make a difference in this vast land. But it was South Africa
that made a difference in me.

When you step outside of yourself and your own concerns to
reach out for others, it will change you. You will be humbled. You
will be inspired. More than anything and more than ever, you will
be overwhelmed with the feeling that you are part of something
much bigger than yourself. Not only that, you will also realize that
you can make a contribution. Everything you do to make someone
else's life better makes your life more meaningful.

After our first few days in South Africa, I came to understand
why John Pingo was so dedicated and driven to help me deliver my
message of hope and faith around his country. He had seen more
than I'd ever seen. I'd led a very self-centered and selfish existence,
I realized; the demanding boy with no arms or legs could not con-
ceive that anyone suffered as much as he.

Since that trip I've never felt the same in a grocery store. The abundance of food even in my neighborhood grocery is beyond the imagination of the orphans and slum dwellers I met in South Africa. Even today I reflect on that trip when I'm feeling pampered in an air-conditioned office, or when I'm given a cool drink; such simple comforts are rarities in that part of the world.

Aaron, who is now a high school math and science teacher in Australia, still talks about what a reality check that trip was. We were saddened at some sights, but amazed by so much else. We agree that it was the best trip of our lives. We both came home wondering, *What can we do to ease the suffering of others? What is the best way to contribute? How could I ever live the same way, knowing that people are suffering so much?*

You don't have to travel far to find someone in need of help. In fact, our trip to South Africa made us more aware of the needy people in our own community and our own country. You can easily find places to give of your time, your talents, or your money at your local churches, nursing homes, the American Red Cross, the Salvation Army, homeless shelters, food banks, and soup kitchens. Whatever you can share will make a difference; whether it is money, your time, your resources, or your network of friends and co-workers.

That first trip to South Africa made me so excited about kicking off my mission that I gave away a good portion of my savings, $20,000; while we were there we raised another $20,000 and gave that away too! We spent entire days buying presents for orphans, feeding them, and stocking up on books and blankets and beds. We gave the orphanages television sets and DVD players, donating funds through a half-dozen charitable networks.

Twenty thousand dollars is still a considerable amount of money in my book, but looking back, I wish I'd had more to give. Just being able to affect a few lives in a few places gave me a greater sense of fulfillment than I'd ever known. My mum wasn't too happy when I returned from South Africa with "nothing" in my savings account, but she saw that my life was enriched beyond measure on that journey.

MIRACLES IN THE MAKING

One of the most emotionally raw and unforgettable scenes from our South Africa trip came when I spoke at a certain church. Hundreds of sick, disabled, and dying people had lined up to seek a healing miracle there. Normally I make a few joking references to my lack of limbs, just to put people at ease. In this church, no one laughed! They were not there for humor. They were there for healing. They wanted miracles.

Every single night they came to this church in neck braces, on crutches, and in wheelchairs with hope for a healing. Two people with AIDS had been dragged on mattresses to the church. Others had walked four and five hours to get there. The back of the church was lined with crutches and wheelchairs that were said to have been left by those who'd been healed. My brother and I talked to a man whose leg and foot were swollen to nearly twice their normal size. He was in agony, but he'd walked to this church to be healed.

Everyone wishes for the power to heal those in pain. I've certainly done my share of praying for a miracle to give me arms and legs. But my request has never been granted, and most of the people we met at that South African church did not get their miracles either. But that does not mean miracles cannot occur. My life may well qualify as a miracle someday, given that I've been able to reach so many diverse audiences, speaking words of faith and inspiration. The fact that this Australian Christian of Serbian descent with no limbs has received invitations to speak from government leaders in Costa Rica, Colombia, Egypt, and China is no small miracle. I've met with Pope Shenouda III of the Coptic Church and with the grand imam Sheikh Mohammed Sayed Tantawi, not to mention with leaders of the Church of Latter-Day Saints. My life is testimony to the fact that there are no limits other than those we impose upon ourselves!

Living without limits means knowing that you always have something to give, something that might ease the burden of others. Even small kindnesses and a few dollars can have a powerful impact. After the terrible earthquake in Haiti in 2010, the American Red Cross quickly set up a program for people to help right away. They made it possible to donate ten dollars by taking a cell phone and texting "HAITI" to the number 90999.

Now, ten dollars doesn't seem like much, and texting it didn't take much effort. It was a small act of charity. But if you were one of those who participated, you made a huge difference. The last time I checked, according to the Red Cross, more than three million people made ten-dollar donations to Haiti on their cell phones. As a result, the Red Cross had received more than $32 million to finance its efforts to help the people of Haiti!

DO WHAT YOU LOVE TO BENEFIT OTHERS

Today my Life Without Limbs nonprofit organization helps support more than ten different charities, including the Apostolic Christian Church Foundation, which sends missionaries around the world; it operates orphanages and churches, including Bombay Teen Challenge in India, which I wrote about earlier in the book. We also partner with Joni and Friends to give away refurbished wheelchairs to people in need.

You can take whatever you love to do, and do it for the benefit of others. Do you play tennis? Ride a bike? Love to dance? Turn your favorite activity into philanthropy: a tennis tournament to benefit your local YMCA, a bike ride for the Boys and Girls Club, or a dance marathon to buy clothing for needy kids.

Hilary Lister loves sailing. At thirty-seven, she decided to try to sail solo around the island of Great Britain. She planned the forty-day sailing trip as a benefit for her charity, Hilary's Dream Trust, which helps disabled and disadvantaged adults learn to sail. She believes sailing can boost the spirits and confidence of people with disabilities.

Hilary's belief in the healing power of sailing is based on personal experience. She has not had the use of her arms or legs since the age of fifteen because of a progressive neurological disorder. A quadriplegic with a degree from Oxford, she sails her custom-outfitted boat using a "sip and puff" system with three straws to operate the controls. One straw controls the tiller, while the others help her steer. She is the first quadriplegic sailor to solo-sail across the English Channel and around Britain.

ONE PERSON AT A TIME

Two years after our amazing experience in South Africa, I got an invitation to speak in Indonesia. The invitation came by e-mail from a gentleman in Perth whose nickname was Han-Han. He was of Chinese descent and pastor of a group of Indonesian churches in Australia.

Upon receiving his e-mail, I called Han-Han, and we spent hours on the phone discussing his proposal. He said my ministry was well known in Indonesia because of my DVDs and videos on the Internet. He offered to set up a speaking tour that would include appearances before tens of thousands of people each weekend. My parents and I prayed over his proposal, and they agreed that I should go, giving their blessings.

I never grow tired of seeing new parts of the world and meeting diverse people, experiencing their cultures and foods. Han-Han had put together a very demanding speaking schedule for me, and I began to have concerns about the rigorous timetable, especially when I discovered that the caregiver they'd provided for me didn't speak English. The language barrier became a huge problem when I developed a digestive virus. My caregiver's inability to understand me and my lack of fingers to gesture and give hand signs led to some very frustrating situations.

My hosts staged a very thoughtful party to celebrate my twenty-third birthday, but my stomach and I were not exactly in the mood for the festivities. I was in so much pain at one point that I prayed for God's help. As I did so, I envisioned Jesus on the cross, and my pain subsided. I then thanked God and enjoyed the rest of my party. The next day I received medical attention, and my condition improved dramatically before I returned to Australia.

A few years later Han-Han invited me to return to Indonesia for another speaking tour. This time I provided my own caregiver and stuck to bottled water with no ice. A businessman in Indonesia, whom we knew as Pa Chokro, arranged for me to speak to nearly forty thousand people at stadium appearances in five cities. The events were also broadcast on television.

One Sunday morning, after I had done three speaking engagements at a church, we took a break since I had three events that evening. I was hungry and tired but decided to address the hunger first. We found a Chinese restaurant near my last speaking venue. A group of local leaders and sponsors of our tour accompanied us. We walked in, with my caregiver Vaughan carrying me.

The restaurant was not fancy, little more than a concrete floor with wooden tables and chairs. Just as we were seated, a young woman came up to the door and leaned against its frame. She was weeping and speaking in Indonesian directly to me. I felt a wave of compassion for her. I had no idea what she was saying, but I could see that she was gesturing at me and in need of a hug.

The businessmen and community leaders with me seemed to be touched by her words. They explained that this woman, Esther, had grown up in a tin-roofed shanty made of cardboard. She lived with her mother and two siblings at the edge of a garbage dump, where they foraged for food each day and collected bits of plastic to sell to the recycling factory. She had a strong faith in God, but when her father left the family, Esther despaired and considered suicide. She believed that her life wasn't worth living.

Upset over the departure of her father, she considered taking her life. She prayed, telling God that she could no longer go to church. That same day her pastor showed the congregation one of my DVDs. It was a black-marketed copy, one of 150,000 made illegally and sold in Indonesia.

When I'd first learned from Han-Han that so many of my DVDs had been pirated and sold, I responded, "Don't worry about it, praise God." I cared more about people hearing my message than about making profits. Even on the black market, God was at work, as Esther would confirm.

Through an interpreter, Esther told me that my DVD had inspired her to reject despair. She came to find a purpose and to have hope. She felt that "if Nick can trust in God, then I can too." She prayed for a job and fasted for six months. She'd found the job in that same Chinese restaurant, which brought us together!

After hearing this story, I gave Esther a hug and asked her what her plans were. She had decided that even though she had little money and worked fourteen hours a day, she would prepare herself to be a children's minister. She hoped to attend a Bible college, even though she wasn't sure how that could happen given her situation. She was living in the restaurant, sleeping on the floor because she couldn't afford a place to live.

I nearly fell off my chair at that revelation. I hadn't felt really comfortable about eating in the place. I couldn't imagine this poor woman sleeping there. I encouraged her to find a different place to live and to pursue her dream to be a children's minister.

One of the members of our group was a pastor. After Esther returned to her work, he told me that the local Bible college was very expensive, and it had a twelve-month waiting list just to take the entrance exam, which very few applicants passed.

A steaming plate full of food was placed in front of me, but I'd lost my appetite. I kept thinking of this poor woman sleeping on the floor. As the rest of the group prayed in thanks for the meal, I prayed for Esther. My prayers were answered almost immediately. The pastor seated next to me said that his church could provide Esther with living accommodations if I contributed the security deposit. I asked if Esther could afford to pay her rent, and the pastor assured me that she could handle it. So I agreed. I was very excited to tell Esther, but before she returned to our table, one of the businessmen said that he would make the down payment himself.

I told him I wanted to do my part, but I appreciated his offer.

Just then another of our party spoke up. "I am the president of the Bible College," he said. "I will allow Esther to take the entrance exam this week, and if she passes, I will see that she gets a scholarship."

God's plan unfolded before my eyes. Esther scored 100 percent on the entrance exam. She graduated from the Bible college in November 2008. She is now the youth director for a children's ministry in one of Indonesia's largest churches, and she has plans to create an orphanage in her community.

Throughout this book I've been telling you about the power of purpose. Esther's story is a testament to that power. This woman had nothing but a sense of purpose and faith in God. Her purpose and her faith created a powerful magnetic field that attracted me and an entire team of people willing to buy into her dream.

THE POWER OF PURPOSE AND FAITH

I am humbled by Esther, her powerful sense of purpose, her undying hope for a better life, her faith in God, her self-love, her positive attitude, her fearlessness and resilience, her willingness to take risks, and her ability to reach out to others.

Esther's story amazes and inspires me. I hope you feel the same way. My purpose in writing this book has been to light the flames of faith and hope inside you so that you too can live a life without limits. Your circumstances may be difficult. You may have challenges with your health, your finances, or your relationships. But with a sense of purpose, faith in your future, and determination to never give up, you can overcome any obstacle.

Esther did it. You can too. When I was growing up, my lack of limbs often seemed like an insurmountable burden, but my "disability" has proven to be a blessing in many, many ways because I learned to follow God's path.

You may face many trials too, but you should know that wherever you feel weakness, God is strong. He took me from disabled to enabled and instilled in me a passion for sharing my stories and my faith to help others cope with their own challenges.

I realized that my purpose was to turn my struggles into lessons that glorify God and inspire others. He blessed me as a blessing to others. Distribute your own blessings with enthusiasm, and know that whatever you do will be multiplied many times. In all things God works for the best for those who love Him. He loves you, and I love you too.

Christians often are told that we are "the hands and feet of Christ" on earth. If I took that literally, I might feel a bit left out. Instead, I take it spiritually. I serve Him by touching as many lives as I can through my testimony and my example. My goal is to reflect the love of Christ for us all. He has given us life so that we might share our gifts with each other. This fills me with joy, and it should fill you with joy too. I hope that the stories and messages in this book have helped and inspired you to find your purpose, to be hopeful, to have faith, to love yourself, to have a positive attitude, and to be fearless, unstoppable, accepting of change, trustworthy, open to opportunities, willing to take risks, and be charitable to others.

Please stay in touch with me and share your stories and thoughts on the book by visiting me online at NickVujicic.com, also known as LifeWithoutLimbs.org and AttitudeIsAltitude.com.

Remember this: God has a truly great purpose for your life! Live it without limits!

With love and faith,
Nick

Personal Action Plan

I n life a plan truly resembles a map: Without a destination or goal, and some clear directions of how to proceed, chances are we will never arrive at where we want to go. If you take some time to work through the questions and exercises on the pages that follow, you will have the "map" that will take you to your own ridiculously good life without limits.

PERSONAL ACTION PLAN #1

Reading Assignment—Chapter One: "If You Can't Get a Miracle, Become One"

Finding your purpose is the first important step in living a life without limits. I've shared how I found happiness and a deep sense of purpose despite difficult circumstances—and I invite you to allow God to guide you in discovering your purpose. I've also shared how valuable you are as God's special creation and that you have something significant to contribute no matter what challenges you face.

Inspiration from Nick

"I have a choice. You have a choice. We can choose to dwell on disappointments and shortcomings... to be bitter, angry, or sad. Or when faced with hard times and hurtful people, we can choose to learn from the experience and move forward, taking responsibility for our own happiness."

Review

- How do you think grasping my value as "God's creation" helps me handle my circumstances and not put limits on how God can work through me?

- Why is it so important for each of us to choose to learn from our experiences and take responsibility for our happiness rather than giving up on our dreams, dwelling on disappointments and shortcomings, and being bitter, angry, or sad?

- As I shared my insights, I mentioned that in "Garbage City" in Egypt I saw people "not only surviving but thriving." What or who helps me and other people to thrive despite incredible suffering?

The Plan

1. Despite my unique challenges, I believe my life has no limits. What challenges are you facing, and what limitations have you either placed on your life or allowed others to place on it? Write these out and reflect on them.

2. Write out your answers to these questions: How do I really feel about myself? How do I believe God views me? In what ways might God work through me to make a significant contribution no matter what my circumstances may be?

3. In what ways might believing that you have power over how your life story will turn out help you to discover the difference you can make in the world?

Action Steps

1. Consider your challenges—including those that have not been your fault or within your power to stop—then list three

specific actions you can take to learn from your experience and begin taking responsibility for your own happiness.

2. How will realizing that you are destined to serve God's purpose—that He created you out of love, and that He continues to love you—provide your life with purpose?

3. Write out three ways in which you can "move forward," "start writing the first chapter" of an adventurous and love-filled life, and keep on striving for a better life rather than giving up or worrying.

PERSONAL ACTION PLAN #2

Reading Assignment—Chapter Two: "No Arms, No Legs, No Limits"

Maintaining hope for the future during difficult times plays a key role in living life without limits. Having experienced hopelessness, I shared how I came to recognize my value and gave practical suggestions on cultivating and embracing a hope-filled life in your journey to live life without limits.

Inspiration from Nick

"Only God knows how our lives will unfold. Hope is His gift to us, a window to look through. We cannot know the future He has planned for us. Trust in Him, keep hope in your heart, and even when faced with the worst, do whatever you can to prepare yourself for the best!"

Review

- What is hope, as I defined it, and what role does God have in our discovering and unleashing the incredible power of a human's spirit?

- Where have I found hope amid suffering—such as the caring ways in which people reach out to help others after a calamity?

• Why do you think I so strongly emphasize that hope is a catalyst that motivates us to take specific actions, such as refusing to give up and keep pushing rather than quitting?

The Plan

1. What role does hope have in giving each of us the courage to pursue our dreams and not doubt our ability to meet whatever challenges come your way?

2. As I worked through my negative thoughts and suicidal despair, what did I realize about myself and God—and the importance of confiding in other people who can provide help?

Action Steps

1. Make two columns. In the first, write down temporary and selfish ways by which people try to sustain themselves during difficult times (e.g., drugs, workaholism, etc.). In the second, write down some sources of hope that I—and perhaps you—

have discovered (e.g., the promise of heaven, God's goodness). What can you begin doing today to cultivate lasting hope in your life and share hope with other people? Write down three specific ways by which you will help to bring hope into the lives of people within your sphere of influence.

2. Every day for the next four days, make a deliberate choice to allow hope to live in your heart, to believe that your days will change for the better, to persevere rather than giving up on your dreams. Also write down any recurring false or negative beliefs and thoughts about yourself, and God, that hinder you from remaining positive and staying focused on solutions rather than problems.

PERSONAL ACTION PLAN #3

Reading Assignment—Chapter Three: "Full Assurance in the Heart"

Having faith in God and the infinite possibilities will keep you moving toward a life without limits. In this action plan, I share my journey of faith and encourages each of you to recognize various types of faith that are part of each day. Through my faith in God, I face each day with confidence and place my future in God's hands.

Inspiration from Nick

"I talk about FAITH as an acronym: **F**ull **A**ssurance **I**n **T**he **H**eart. I may not be able to produce evidence for all that I believe in, but I feel fully assured in my heart that I am much closer to the truth by living with faith than I would be by living in despair."

Review

- What are some of the forms of faith that I mention, and why is it important to recognize them?

- What is a possibilitarian, and what characteristics does this kind of person have?

- Why is patience a key part of overcoming challenges?

The Plan

1. What are some areas in which you demonstrate faith each day, and why is it important for you to recognize this faith

as you face challenges—sometimes seemingly insurmountable ones?

2. How is life different for people who trust that God's plan for them will be revealed in time versus people who do not walk in faith and do not trust that God is looking out for them?

3. Why is it important to recognize that sometimes you won't get the answers you seek right away and have to walk by faith?

Action Steps

1. Do you find it easy or difficult to believe that if you do everything possible to achieve your dreams, your efforts will be rewarded? Which situations and people have encouraged or discouraged you in this area?

2. List several people who may be willing to lend you an encouraging hand and serve as your guides in accomplishing your goals in life. Then talk with them about it. If you don't have people to list, go find several! Also, choose one person who needs encouragement and either call or visit him or her.

3. Choose one area in life and take specific steps to pursue your dream, just as I chose to get on a surfboard and learned to surf—and choose to respond in positive ways no matter which obstacles you face.

PERSONAL ACTION PLAN #4

Reading Assignment—Chapter Four: "Love the Perfectly Imperfect You"

Recognizing that God loves you unconditionally is an important step in self-love and self-acceptance. Sadly, many pressures move us toward bitterness and self-loathing. In order to shine from within, we each must look inside for strength and look above, to God—our ultimate source of strength and love. We are bombarded with messages that we need to have a certain look, drive a certain car, and maintain a certain lifestyle in order to be fulfilled, loved, appreciated, or considered successful. We must not allow other people to determine our value.

Inspiration from Nick

"Instead of dwelling on your imperfections, your failings, or your mistakes, focus on your blessings and the contribution you can make, whether it's a talent, knowledge, wisdom, creativity, hard work, or a nurturing soul."

Review

- Why did I (and so many other people) have a hard time accepting themselves just the way they are—living life burdened with feelings that they don't measure up?

- What pressures do teens and young adults, especially, face that can lead them to be depressed and suicidal?

- Why, according to me, must we base our self-love and self-acceptance on God's unconditional love, and in what ways is this perspective different from loving ourselves in a self-absorbed, conceited, self-satisfied way?

The Plan

1. Why is it vital that we accept ourselves as we are rather than disliking or even hating ourselves for our flaws, and what steps can we take to gain a healthy and realistic view of ourselves?

2. Why is it so easy in today's culture to lack unconditional love and self-acceptance—to hang on to the hurt rather than the supportive words, to focus on our shortcomings rather than positive aspects of ourselves?

Action Steps

1. Evaluate your life so far. Write down the times when other people put you down and the times when you compared yourself to other people and didn't seem to measure up. Now write down how those people and situations influenced your view of yourself. Finally, journal about how you might strengthen your view of yourself—including facing the ways in which you have not loved or accepted yourself as God's creation.

2. Using a concordance or other biblical resource, look up verses on God's unconditional love, mercy, and forgiveness for you. As a start, look up John 3:16, Romans 8:38–39, Hebrews 4:16, John 10:10, 1 John 1:9, and Ephesians 1:7.

3. Take time to find one feature that you love about yourself—a physical characteristic, talent, trait, or something else. Then, thank God that He has given this to you and ask Him to help you recognize His unconditional love for you just the way you are.

4. In what ways might you overcome doubts about your self-worth or your inability to love yourself as you are—such as volunteering at a soup kitchen? Write down several options, and arrange to reach out to someone in need within the next few days by using your talents, brains, and personality to make life better for someone else.

PERSONAL ACTION PLAN #5

Reading Assignment—Chapter Five: "Attitude Is Altitude"

Without a positive attitude, we cannot rise above our challenges. Each of us views the world through our own unique perspectives or attitudes based on our beliefs. Since our decisions and actions are based on these attitudes, it's vital that when what we've been doing isn't working, we adjust our attitudes and change our lives.

Inspiration from Nick

"You and I may have absolutely no control over what happens to us, but we can control how we respond. If we choose the right attitude, we can rise above whatever challenges we face…. Optimism is empowering—it gives you control over your emotions. Pessimism weakens your will and allows your moods to control your actions."

Review

- What practical suggestions did I offer concerning "attitude adjustment"?

- Which attitudes do I believe are the most powerful? Why?

The Plan

1. Which "attitude adjustment" suggestions did you find most helpful? Why?

2. What is required for us to rise above the challenges we have faced and pursue our dreams?

3. Why are the attitudes of gratitude, action, empathy, and forgiveness so empowering?

Action Steps

1. Which specific attitudes in your life need "adjustment," and what will you begin doing today to accomplish this?

2. Take specific steps to express each of the following attitudes: gratitude, action, empathy, forgiveness. Keep track of your successes, and work hard to make each of them a natural expression of who you are becoming.

3. Write down the names of any persons whom you need to forgive—and then make a conscious decision to ask for God's help to be committed to allow for a heart-change to happen, sometimes slowly, sometimes quickly. Either way, stay committed to wanting to forgive with all your heart one day. That's a great start!

PERSONAL ACTION PLAN #6

Reading Assignment—Chapter Six: "Armless But Not Harmless"

In this personal action plan, I focus on courageously confronting fears—on being fearless as you pursue your dream. Using stories from my life, I show how I discovered that I could use fear to motivate myself and how I no longer allow my fears to control my actions.

Inspiration from Nick

"So many people are handicapped by fear of failure, fear of making mistakes, fear of making a commitment, even fear of success. It's inevitable that fears will come knocking on your door. You don't have to let them in."

Review

- In what ways can fear—a powerful emotion—hinder us from being who we want to be and going for our dreams?

- How did I draw on my fear of public speaking to become even more effective?

The Plan

1. In which specific areas have you had too much fear and consequently avoided facing your fears, surrendered to them, and limited yourself? If you were not limited by any fears, what dreams would you like to chase? Why?

2. What has happened when you, like me, have sometimes allowed your fears to control your actions? (Be honest!) How do you feel about this? Why?

3. How might you, like me, learn to welcome your fear as a source of energy and motivation to take positive action that puts you closer to your dream?

Action Steps

1. Draw three columns on a sheet of paper. In the first, write down the fears you have experienced—from as far back as you can remember. In the second, write down how each fear influenced you. In the third, write down real-life experiences in which you persevered and overcame fear-related challenges. If any of these fears still influence you today, draw on Nick's suggestions and commit to taking specific action to confront and overcome these fears.

2. Within your circles of influence—at school, at work, in your neighborhood—which person(s) might you sincerely encourage

to go for the life they want and not let fear keep them from working toward their dreams? Ask God to guide you in connecting with this person and sharing what you have learned about facing fears and pursuing an enjoyable and fulfilling life.

PERSONAL ACTION PLAN #7

Reading Assignment—Chapter Seven: "Don't Let Your Face Plant Grow Roots"

Each of us faces failure. The best of us fail, and the rest of us fail. I faced this challenge early and encourage others to recognize their problems, work harder, be resilient, and keep searching for creative solutions no matter how many times we fail.

Inspiration from Nick

"Losing doesn't make you a loser any more than striking out makes a great baseball player a benchwarmer. As long as you stay in the game and keep swinging, you can still be a slugger."

Review

- In what ways do our challenges help make us stronger, better, and more prepared for success?

- What reactions do you have to this quote from Thomas Merton?
  "A humble man is not afraid of failure. In fact, he is not afraid
  of anything, even of himself, since perfect humility implies perfect
  confidence in the power of God before Whom no other power has any
  meaning and for Whom there is no such thing as an obstacle."

The Plan

1. Ponder my four lessons of failure and how they relate to your
   unique situation and experiences.

2. I shared a story about David, who transferred his skills from
   golf courses to managing businesses. In what ways might you
   need to do this—and how might doing this deepen your
   character?

Action Steps

1. Write down three or four specific ways in which you will buck
   up, stay strong, and keep pursuing your dream(s). Then begin

to apply what you learned in this chapter—patiently doing your best and allowing God to do the rest.

2. Read the Bible story of Joseph in Genesis 39–41, then write out some lessons concerning his struggles and ultimate ascension to a position of great power. (For example, what does this true story reveal about the relationship that sometimes develops between success and pain?)

PERSONAL ACTION PLAN #8

Reading Assignment—Chapter Eight: "The New Bloke in the Bushes"

We all experience change and must learn to master it. To handle changes positively, we must envision what lies on the other side. We need to have hope and faith in God and in our abilities to find something better. As I discovered, making positive changes has five necessary stages.

Inspiration from Nick

"There are two major types of change that tend to challenge us and disrupt our day-to-day lives. The first happens to us. The second happens within us. We can't control the first, but we can and should control the second."

Review

- As I faced major changes, how did I respond, and what kinds of things did I learn about myself, God, and other people?

- What five necessary stages does someone who makes a positive change pass through—and which one(s) did you identify with most?

The Plan

1. When have you felt trapped in circumstances, then discovered that the only trap was your own lack of vision, lack of courage, or failure to see that you had better options?

2. Review the five necessary stages of positive change, then consider how they relate to you and your unique situation. (An example: "I recognize that I need to overcome my laziness and fear and meet more people." Or "It's time for me to finally go find a better job instead of just complaining about it.")

Action Steps

1. In light of what you just decided to do, write down which action(s) you will take immediately—and start doing it! Be willing to "let go of the old" and keep climbing up!

2. Starting today, how will you embrace change that elevates your life and be a force for change that uplifts the lives of other people too? Think about and/or journal about how you can accomplish both of these goals.

PERSONAL ACTION PLAN #9

Reading Assignment—Chapter Nine: "Trust Others, More or Less"

"We all need supportive relationships. We all must engage with kindred spirits. To do that effectively, we must build trust and prove ourselves trustworthy. We must understand that most people instinctively act out of self-interest, but if you show them that you are interested in them and invested in their success, most will do the same for you."

Inspiration from Nick

"The art of reading people, relating to them, engaging with them, and stepping into their shoes, knowing whom to trust and how to be trustworthy, is critical to your success and happiness. Few people succeed without the ability to build relationships based on mutual understanding and trust. We all need not just someone to love but also friends, mentors, role models, and supporters who buy into our dreams and help us achieve them."

Review

- Why are primary people skills vital in building bonds of trust and mutually supportive relationships?

- As I defined them, what are the differences between a mentor, role model, and fellow traveler—and what important role does each fulfill?

The Plan

1. Which of the eight primary people skills that I mentioned do you find easiest to use? hardest to use? Why?

2. Why do you think I believe that the willingness and humility to ask for help when you need it is a people skill often disdained or overlooked? Do you tend to view asking for help as a strength or a weakness? Why?

Action Steps

1. It's easy to read about some people skills, and more difficult to acknowledge that you are not particularly great at using some

of them! Write down some reasons that may be keeping you from really developing strong people skills (e.g., fear of closeness, being afraid of criticism, etc.).

2. Ask God to guide you, in His perfect timing, to someone with whom you can provide such blessings of relationship as a helpful hand, honest advice, mentoring, encouragement, ongoing guidance.

PERSONAL ACTION PLAN #10

Reading Assignment—Chapter Ten: "An Equal Opportunity Hugger"

Opportunities come to us during even the most difficult times. In fact, such times can be blessings in disguise by motivating us to invest in our futures by preparing with hard work, dedicating ourselves to our goals, and watching for the right times to make "the leap." In this action plan, I also provide practical principles that will help you evaluate opportunities and choose those that meet your goals and values.

Inspiration from Nick

"To pursue your dreams you have to take action. Move it or lose it. Act or be acted upon. If you don't have what you want, consider creating what you want. God will light the path. Your chance of a lifetime, the door to your dreams is open. Your path to a purpose may present itself at any moment. Be ready for it. Do all you need to do. Learn all you need to know. If no one comes knocking, beat down a few doors. One day you'll step into the life you desire."

Review

- What did I mean by these words: "You have to seize upon every thread and weave a rope you can climb," and why does this approach to life lead to new opportunities?

- Which actions did I recommend to combat feelings of despair and bitterness?

The Plan

1. What steps might you start taking today to use your challenges to lift you up and use opportunities to build momentum and create a life you love?

2. In what ways should your purpose and values guide you as you consider opportunities and choose those that will best serve your ultimate goals and not cause you to slip and fall?

Action Steps

1. Reflect on the mark you wish to make in the world and how you want to be remembered. (You might write this down and keep rereading it to remind you of your purpose and values.)

2. Write down your purpose—at least the one that is growing within your heart and mind—and what you value most highly,

then determine how you will use it in evaluating opportunities that take you another step closer to your dream. Do you think that I believe that the greatest purpose is to know God? Why could this be true?

3. Reread some of the suggestions on widening your network, which in turn will increase opportunities (pages 190–191), then take steps to do some of them.

PERSONAL ACTION PLAN #11

Reading Assignment—Chapter Eleven: "The Ridiculous Rules"

In this action plan, I encourage each of you to do something ridiculous at least once a day, whether it's risking looking ridiculous to pursue your dream or simply having ridiculous fun. Be willing to take risks and dare to be called crazy by those who doubt your genius.

Inspiration from Nick

"You can't be a winner unless you're willing to face defeat."

Review

- Why is being playful, taking risks, and laughing at yourself an important part of the journey of living life without limits?

- What are my "Ridiculous Rules," and how did you respond as you read each of them? (Be honest!)

- What differences exist between ridiculous risk and stupid risk, and how does a person prepare before taking ridiculous risks?

The Plan

1. In what way(s) have you slipped into the "someday" mentality and limited your opportunities to laugh, play, and enjoy ridiculous fun?

2. Why does taking moderate risks from time to time make a person feel alive?

3. If you could do several activities that would provide moderate risk and be great fun, what would you choose? Why?

Action Steps

1. Which steps will you take right now in order to enjoy life more and be more empowered to live out your dream?

2. How might you cultivate relationships with people who take ridiculous risks and enjoy ridiculous fun? (Hint: What about trying a new sport, learning a new skill...?)

3. Set aside time to be "lost" or totally engaged in a favorite activity with ridiculous enthusiasm—working on a car, playing a board game, painting, running a marathon, building something... And make it happen!

PERSONAL ACTION PLAN #12

Reading Assignment—Chapter Twelve: "Make Giving Your Mission"

Through various circumstances, I came to understand the importance of reaching out to other people and sharing the love of Jesus through kind, practical ways. This personal action plan invites you to show compassion toward other people, whether you have a lot or a little, whether you have many skills or just one. If you make a positive difference in just one person's life, you've done a great service! And be prepared to receive many blessings, too, including a more meaningful life.

Inspiration from Nick

"The more I dwelled on my own challenges, the worse I felt, but when I changed my focus to serving the needs of someone else, it lifted my spirits and helped me understand that no one suffers alone."

Review

- Why are simple acts of kindness so powerful?

- What do I emphasizes about God and His blessings when we make ourselves available to do good works that honor Him?

The Plan

1. Reflect on your skill set and abilities, then write down ways in which you do whatever you love to do in order to show kindness to other people. (For example: visiting nursing homes, helping in a Habitat for Humanity project, working at a food bank or homeless shelter, etc.)

2. Why is it important for people to draw on the awesome love of God when doing things for other people?

Action Steps

1. Knowing that even the simplest act of kindness can make a positive difference in someone's life, show kindness to one specific person today. Whatever God has given you, share it in ways to benefit others.

2. In light of the stories I've shared, what will you do to be "the hands and feet of Christ" each day, reflecting His love to other people? And if you do not yet know Jesus personally, what will you do to discover Jesus—His love for you, His promises to you, His plan for your life? (Hints: read the book of John in the New Testament; talk with a local pastor; seek out a follower of Jesus with whom you can discuss various topics; do on-line Bible study; etc.)

Acknowledgments

GOD: The Father, Son, and Holy Spirit.

The ones who I strive to make proud, my pillars of strength, Dad and Mum. I love you so much! Thank you for everything! To my brother, my true first best friend and rock, Aaron, and my sister-in-law, Michelle. To my inspiration to never compromise in integrity and to be the best I can be, my dear sister, Michelle.

To my Vujicic grandparents, Vladimir and Nada, now resting in eternal peace, who encouraged me to believe and be disciplined. To my grandma, who I'll get to know better in heaven, Anica Radojevic. To my ninety-three-year-old grandpa, Dragoljub Radojevic, and his wife, Ana, who taught me to never add to or subtract from the Gospel.

My love and thanks to all of my uncles and aunties, first, second, and third cousins, and other family members. In loving memory of Bosko Zunic, Roy Zunic, Martin Poljak, Joshua Vujicic, Steve Nenadov, and Barney Nenadov.

The board of directors for Life Without Limbs (USA): Batta Vujicic, David Price, Dan'l Markham, Don McMaster, and their wives and families. Ignatius Ho, a director on the board of the Hong Kong chapter of Life Without Limbs and my founding friend, George

Miksa. A huge thank you to the prudent, diligent, and loyal staff of Life Without Limbs for all their love and support. The volunteering international co-ordinators for Life Without Limbs. The Apostolic Christian Church of the Nazarean, and a very special thanks to Joni and Friends Ministry who have always been there for our ministry, and me personally. The team of Attitude is Altitude, and my mentors and coaches who always believed in me.

A big thank-you to my literary agents with great patience and faith in me, Jan Miller and Nena Madonia of Dupree Miller & Associates, and their team. Also to my writer, Wes Smith, who has done an absolutely incredible job at helping me put this together and working around our hectic touring. To the Crown Publishing Group and the entire team, thank you. Special thanks to Michael Palgon, Trace Murphy, and Karin Schulze.

Finally, a huge thank-you to all my friends who have loved, supported, and prayed for me along the way. To all of you who are reading, I want to also acknowledge your support as you help spread this message of hope to your family and friends. Thank you very much!

Resources

GET PLUGGED INTO PHILANTHROPY

I encourage you to be just as creative as Hilary Lister in finding ways to give and support others. The latest trends in philanthropy include micro-volunteering and micro-action, which are spin-offs from successful micro-lending programs that have provided millions and millions of dollars in small loans. If you have a cell phone and a few extra minutes, you can reach out as a micro-volunteer to take micro-action to help a worthy cause or a person in need.

A social entrepreneurial enterprise called the Extraordinaries operates a for-profit service for those who are willing to do good using their smartphones or their Web browsers. The idea is that while many people can't give up an entire day to do good deeds, they can do a little here and there, while commuting by rail or bus, waiting in line, or during breaks at work. The Extraordinaries Web site 4(http://www.beextra.org) and smartphone application hooks those people up so they can do benevolent work in small bites.

Some of the good deeds that the Extraordinaries can help you perform, according to their Web site, include recording an audio version of a book just a few pages at a time for a group that distributes audiobooks to the disabled; translating a nonprofit's Web site into a foreign language; recording pothole locations for your town; identifying birds for the Cornell Lab of Ornithology; tagging images for the Smithsonian; identifying and mapping good and safe places for kids to play; or reviewing congressional bills for hidden pork.

The company plans to make money by charging organizations a fee for each task performed by its micro-volunteers, a movement that uses technology and crowd sourcing to do little things that add up to a lot of good. It's cutting-edge philanthropy that uses the Internet and social networking to make the planet a better place. Here are just a few Web sites where you can plug into the "Giving Grid" from your laptop or smart phone.

CAUSECAST.COM

Multimillionaire tech entrepreneur Ryan Scott founded Causecast to help nonprofit and charitable organizations reduce high-cost donation transaction fees that cut into their ability to do good. Causecast accomplishes that mission with innovative methods that include helping donors make contributions via their cell phones by using a "text-to-pay payment system." Causecast has branched out to serve as a link between worthy nonprofits and companies interested in developing cause-marketing campaigns. This $1.5 billion industry involves major companies who want to partner their brands with good causes and support them through donations or shared proceeds.

DONORSCHOOSE.ORG

This education advocacy site encourages "citizen philanthropy" by taking requests for assistance from public schoolteachers across North America looking for everything from pencils for economically disadvantaged students to chemistry lab equipment, musical instruments, and books. You can go to their Web site, choose which request you want to help with, and donate any amount you want. DonorsChoose.org then delivers the materials to the school. They also provide photos of your gift in use at the schools, a thank-you letter from the teacher, and a cost report showing how your money was spent. Larger donors get personal thank-you letters from the students.

AMAZEE.COM

This social-networking site promotes advocacy projects, sort of a Facebook for philanthropists in action. It encourages people who want to be charitable to promote their ideas, recruit fellow believers, and raise money on its global action network. Its members' projects have included building an IT learning center for the poor in Sri Lanka and helping to supply running water to a village in South Africa.

GLOBALGIVING.COM

GlobalGiving's goal is to help donors become doers by connecting them to more than seven hundred prescreened grassroots charity projects, according to its Web site. "From running orphanages and schools, to helping survivors of natural disasters, these people are do-gooders to the core. We connect these 'good idea people' with the 'generous giver people' and help projects of all sizes receive donations of all sizes," the site says.

People with projects post their causes and wish lists on the Web site, and those who wish to make donations can pick and choose those they want to support or become involved in. GlobalGiving also guarantees that 85 percent of each donation is "on-the-ground within 60 days and has an immediate impact."

KIVA.ORG

This Web site connects the needy and the working poor to those willing to loan or give them a little at a time. Billed as "the world's first person-to-person micro-lending website," it allows visitors to browse profiles of its low-income entrepreneurs and then to make small loans of six to twelve months to those selected. Donors are kept updated on the entrepreneur's progress via e-mails, journal updates, and repayment tracking.

A few dollars here and there can add up when millions are willing to give. Kiva.org reports that so far more than $80 million has been distributed from more than a half-million micro-lenders to people in 184 countries. The Web site uses PayPal or credit cards to distribute small loans of $25 or more.

KINDED.COM

The power of the Internet is increasingly being tapped by inventive philanthropists like Daniel Lubetsky, a social entrepreneur and founder of Peace/Works, a "not-only-for-profit" food and condiment company, based in my native Australia, that makes all-natural KIND fruit and nut bars.

Lubetsky created the "kinding" movement to encourage people to surprise others with unexpected acts of kindness, according to his Kinded.com Web site. You can go to the Web site, make your own Kinded card to print out, and then when you do something nice for someone, you pass the card to that person so they can pass it along by doing something nice for someone else. The cards are coded so that they can be tracked online and each person can see the rippling effect of each good deed.

IFWERANTHEWORLD.COM

There are so many creative ways to reach out. A new online project called IfWeRanTheWorld.com encourages individuals, organizations, and corporations to take on worthy causes in small, manageable steps. You can go to the Web site, fill in your suggestion to the phrase *If I ran the world I would . . .* , and then the site's operators hook you up to others willing to find ways to follow through on your idea and pitch in.

NEVER CHAINED

One of our current philanthropic projects at Life Without Limbs takes a similar approach. We are creating the equivalent of an online shelter or youth self-counseling center: a Web site where people can share their stories of both hurt and healing and then help each other find ways to move to a better place emotionally and spiritually.

I was inspired to do this a few years ago when I met a seventeen-year-old girl who'd been raped three years earlier. She told me that she'd had no one to talk to about her terrible experience, but God had healed her heart through prayer. She'd then written a song about the healing, in hope of helping others. "Maybe because of what I went through I can help someone who is thinking about giving up, or maybe I can save a soul," she told me.

Her story inspired me to create this Web site, where her story and her song can be heard by people seeking healing and inspiration. I can't imagine the physical and emotional pain she experienced. I couldn't be there for her when she needed help because I didn't know her then. But I can help her and others tell their stories and heal each other. The Web site is called Never Chained, after the Bible phrase that says "the word of God is never chained."

My plan is to have a two-stage experience for Never Chained. In the first section, visitors will be able to share their stories of need; then on the second page, we will link them to people who want to offer assistance or comfort. I think of it as a social-networking site where those in need can connect to those seeking to make a difference. Our goal is modest: to change the world one person at a time. We are still in the process of developing this Web site. Our goal is to inspire teens to become involved and encouraged in philanthropy. You can check LifeWithoutLimbs.org for any updates not just on this project but on our travels and stories on how people's lives are being transformed.

Links to others you've met in this book:

Dr. Stuart Brown
www.nifplay.org

Reggie Dabbs
www.reggiedabbsonline.com

Bethany Hamilton
www.bethanyhamilton.com

Gabe Murfitt
www.gabeshope.org

Vic & Elsie Schlatter
Apostolic Christian Church Foundation
www.accm.org

Glennis Siverson
www.glennisphotos.com

Joni Eareckson Tada
www.joniandfriends.org

Phil Toth
www.PhilToth.com

SHARE THE INSPIRATION.

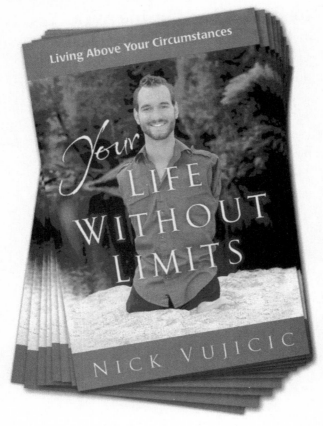

Know someone who could be encouraged by Nick's incredible life? Share the booklet version of *Life Without Limits*. In this short booklet, Nick explores topics like daring to dream, finding purpose, trusting God, overcoming defeat and failure, managing emotions, and avoiding despair. The result is an inspiring summary of how hope changes everything for the better.

No Bully Can Define Who You Are

Born without arms or legs, Nick Vujicic knows what it's like to be different. And he knows what it's like to be bullied—and rise above it. In *Stand Strong*, Nick gives you strategies for responding to the bullies in your life, empowering you to feel more confident than you ever felt before.

Available wherever books and eBooks are sold April 2014.

Read an excerpt from this book and more on
WaterBrookMultnomah.com!

No Arms, No Legs,
NO LIMITS.

Despite being born without arms or legs, Nick Vujicic's challenges have not kept him from enjoying a "ridiculously" good life. When trials come, he focuses on the promise that God is always present. In *Unstoppable* Nick addresses the adversity and difficult circumstances that many people face today and how to respond to these issues. Are you ready to become unstoppable? Let Nick inspire you!

Read an excerpt of this book and more at www.WaterBrookMultnomah.com!

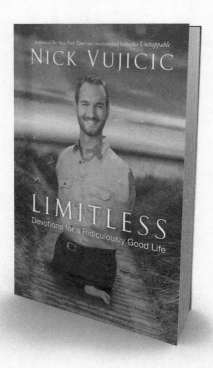